D0546307

Contents

Appetizers and Soups	5
Salads and Gravies	16
Chicken Dishes	24
Turkey Dishes	67
Other Fowl	79
Equivalent Measures	94
Index	95

CHICKEN
TURKEY & FOWL
C·O·O·K·B·O·O·K

GOLDEN APPLE PUBLISHERS

CHICKEN, TURKEY AND FOWL COOKBOOK

A GOLDEN APPLE PUBLICATION/
PUBLISHED BY ARRANGEMENT WITH OTTENHEIMER PUBLISHERS INC.

JUNE 1986

GOLDEN APPLE IS A TRADEMARK OF GOLDEN APPLE PUBLISHERS

ISBN 0-553-19851-3

Appetizers and Soups

Chicken Pâté Cream

Bacon fat
2 tablespoons butter
1½ pounds chicken livers
½ pound unsalted pork fat, ground
2 tablespoons dry sherry
2 tablespoons brandy
½ teaspoon freshly ground pepper
3 green onions or shallots, chopped
1 clove garlic, minced
1½ teaspoons salt

Coat a 7-inch soufflé mold well with cold bacon fat. Melt butter in a skillet. Sauté livers until all the pink has disappeared. Combine livers, pork fat, sherry, brandy, pepper, onions, garlic, and salt and mix well. Place a small amount of liver at a time in blender or food processor, and blend until thoroughly pureed. The blending may take longer than usual as the pork fat is not easily pureed.

Spoon liver mixture into prepared mold and cover with aluminum foil. Place mold in a baking dish. Pour hot water halfway the depth of the mold. Bake in a preheated 350°F oven for 1 hour. Remove from oven and let cool.

Invert onto a serving platter and chill in refrigerator overnight. Serve with French bread or crackers. Makes about 2 cups.

Bartender's Hors d'Oeuvres

12 chicken wings or squab legs	1 cup cornmeal
1 to 2 dozen Brussels sprouts	Salt and pepper
1 cup flour	Oil for deep-frying

Wash and dry chicken wings and Brussels sprouts. Dip them into a mixture of flour, cornmeal, salt, and pepper. Deep-fry in hot oil. approximately 375°F until golden brown. Cool and serve. Makes 4 servings.

Fried Chicken Drumsticks

8 chicken drumsticks	1 egg, beaten
Flour	Fine dry bread crumbs
Salt and pepper	Oil for deep-frying

Dip drumsticks in seasoned flour, then in beaten egg. Finally, coat them in bread crumbs. Heat oil until hot. Fry chicken until golden and tender, about 15 to 20 minutes. Drain well on paper towels. Serve hot or cold. Makes 4 to 8 servings.

Hot Chicken Liver and Sausage Pâté

2 tablespoons butter	¼ teaspoon rosemary
½ pound chicken livers	½ teaspoon allspice
1 teaspoon salt	½ teaspoon freshly ground pepper
¼ cup Madeira	1 pound mild sausage
2 tablespoons cognac	
3 eggs	
2 tablespoons all-purpose flour	

Melt butter in a skillet, then add chicken livers. Sauté until all pink disappears. Cool for about 10 minutes. Combine chicken livers, salt, Madeira, cognac, eggs, flour, and seasonings in blender or food processor. Blend for about 3 minutes or until the mixture is thoroughly pureed. Blend pureed mixture and the sausage thoroughly.

Spoon chicken-liver mixture into a 7-inch pâté mold and cover tightly. Place mold in a larger baking dish and add hot water to half the depth of the mold. Bake in a preheated 350°F oven for 1 hour and 45 minutes.

Unmold onto a serving platter and slice to serve. May be chilled and served cold. Makes 8 to 10 servings.

Chicken-Liver Pâté

2 tablespoons butter	1 tablespoon parsley, finely
½ pound chicken livers	chopped
2 eggs, hard-cooked	¾ teaspoon salt
1 (3-ounce) package cream	⅛ teaspoon pepper
cheese, softened	1 tablespoon cognac

Heat butter in medium frying pan. Cook chicken livers, stirring occasionally, over medium heat 10 minutes or until tender; drain.

Chop livers and eggs a little at a time in food grinder, blender, or food processor.

With wooden spoon, work cheese until light and fluffy. Mix into liver mixture along with remaining ingredients. Refrigerate several hours.

Serve pâté with hot toast or crackers. Makes 1-1/4 cups.

Chicken Wings with Oyster Sauce

2 pounds chicken wings (tips may be removed if you wish)	2 tablespoons soy sauce
	1 tablespoon brown sugar
	2 teaspoons dry sherry
3 slices fresh gingerroot	⅛ teaspoon 5-spice powder
1 clove garlic crushed	(optional)
3 tablespoons oyster sauce	1 cup chicken broth

Place chicken wings in wok and add remaining ingredients. Bring to a boil over moderate heat and simmer, covered, until wings are tender, about 20 minutes. Remove wings and boil hard to evaporate all but about 1/2 cup of sauce. Eat hot, or chill and serve cold for a picnic lunch or as a snack. Makes 4 servings.

Chicken Chowder

Carcass and giblets of 1 chicken	1 teaspoon salt
	1 (1-pound) can cream-style
3 pints boiling water	corn
1 onion, peeled and sliced	2 eggs (1 hard-boiled)
3 stalks celery with leaves, chopped	1 cup flour
	¼ teaspoon salt
1 carrot, peeled and diced	

Fried Chicken Drumsticks

Break up carcass; put with giblets into large kettle. Add boiling water, onion, celery, carrot, and salt; cover. Simmer about 1-1/2 hours. Remove pieces of carcass and giblets. Cut off all meat; return to pan. Add corn; simmer 10 minutes. Add finely chopped, hard-cooked egg; adjust seasoning.

Sift flour and salt together; stir in remaining egg; beat with fork until mixture looks like cornmeal. Drop by spoonfuls into hot soup a few minutes before serving. Makes 5 or 6 servings.

Balnamoon Skink

1	(2½- to 3-pound) chicken	1¼	cups frozen peas
6	cups water	¼	teaspoon ground mace
2	teaspoons salt	2	egg yolks
½	teaspoon pepper	½	cup whipping cream
1	celery root	2	cups shredded leaf lettuce
1	leek, sliced		or outer leaves of an
1	large carrot, peeled and		iceberg lettuce
	sliced		
2	tablespoons parsley,		
	chopped		

Wash chicken well inside and out. Combine chicken, water, salt, and pepper in Dutch oven. Cover; bring to boil over moderate heat. Skim any froth from surface. Reduce heat to low; cook 1 hour.

Clean and cube celery root. Add celery root, leek, and carrot to soup; cook 15 minutes. Remove chicken; cool slightly. Skin; remove from bones; dice. Return chicken to soup. Add parsley, peas, and mace; simmer 8 to 10 minutes.

Beat egg yolks and cream together well in small bowl. Add some of soup to cream mixture; beat well. Add slowly to soup, mixing well. Cook over very low heat 3 minutes. Ladle soup into serving bowls; sprinkle each bowl with some lettuce. Makes 6 servings.

Broth with Liver Dumplings

4	chicken livers	1	tablespoon parsley,
½	small onion		chopped
1	tablespoon chicken fat or	Salt and pepper	
	soft butter	1	tablespoon flour
1	egg, beaten	Approximately 3 tablespoons	
½	teaspoon crumbled dried		dry bread crumbs
	marjoram	5	cups beef or chicken broth

Put chicken livers and onion through food grinder, or chop in food processor. Add fat, egg, and seasonings; mix well. Add flour and bread crumbs; mix. Add enough bread crumbs to form stiff mixture. Refrigerate 1 hour.

Heat broth to boiling in medium saucepan. Form liver mixture into walnut-sized dumplings. Drop into boiling soup; do not crowd. Cook 10 minutes or until dumplings float. Remove with slotted spoon; place in warm soup tureen. Continue until all dumplings are cooked. Strain broth over dumplings.

Serve soup garnished with chopped parsley. Makes 4 servings.

Chicken Liver Wrapped in Bacon

¼ **cup button mushrooms**	**Salt and pepper**
Oil	¾ **pound chicken livers**
1 **level teaspoon dried thyme**	¼ **to ½ pound bacon**

Wipe mushrooms and cut off stalks level with caps. Put them into a shallow bowl and cover with oil; sprinkle with thyme, salt, and pepper. Leave for 1 to 2 hours.

Meanwhile, wash and trim chicken livers. Remove all membranes. Spread the bacon with the back of a knife until it is twice the original length. Cut into pieces. Wrap a chicken liver in each piece of bacon and secure with a wooden cocktail toothpick. Drain mushrooms and put a mushroom, or half a mushroom (if they are large), on the end of each stick. Grill over a hot fire until bacon is crisp and livers cooked. Serve immediately. Makes 4 to 6 servings.

Chicken Liver Wrapped in Bacon

Chicken Noodle Soup

3 pounds chicken, cut up	**½ teaspoon poultry**
1 tablespoon salt	**seasoning**
Water to cover	**1 tablespoon dehydrated**
1 cup carrots, sliced	**parsley flakes**
1½ cups celery with leaves,	**2 cups (about ¼-pound)**
chopped	**uncooked noodles**
½ cup onion, chopped	

Simmer chicken in salted water in covered saucepan until tender. (A frying chicken will take about 45 minutes.) Remove chicken from broth; let sit until cool enough to handle. Remove skin and bones; chop meat.

Skim most fat from broth; measure broth. Add water, if needed, to make 5 cups; bring to boil. Add chicken, vegetables, and poultry seasoning. Simmer, covered, 20 minutes. Add parsley and noodles. Simmer, uncovered, 10 minutes or until noodles are tender. Makes 6 servings.

Giblet Soup

½ pound chicken gizzards	**10 peppercorns**
¼ pound chicken livers	**Salt**
1 pound chicken necks	**1½ tablespoons butter**
Flour seasoned with salt and	**½ cup onions, chopped**
pepper	**1 cup tomatoes, chopped**
Bacon drippings	**½ cup carrots, diced**
2½ quarts water	**½ cup celery, chopped**
4 stalks celery with leaves	**¼ teaspoon pepper**
1 bay leaf	**1 tablespoon lemon juice**

Dredge gizzards, livers, and necks in flour.

Heat bacon drippings in large, heavy kettle until hot. Add giblets; brown on all sides. Add water, celery stalks, bay leaf, peppercorns, and 1 teaspoon salt; bring to boil. Cover and boil gently 1-1/2 hours. Strain stock; set giblets aside to cool.

Heat butter in kettle. Add onions; sauté until golden.

Chop gizzards and livers. Add strained stock, gizzards, livers, tomatoes, carrots, chopped celery, pepper, and salt to taste; cover. Boil gently 30 minutes or until vegetables are tender. Stir in lemon juice. Meat from necks can be added, if desired. Soup can be frozen. Makes about 6 servings.

Chicken Breasts with Celery Salad

Chicken Soup Irish-Style

5 **cups water**	2 **medium potatoes, cubed**
1½ **teaspoons salt**	½ **cup peas**
2 **pounds chicken parts**	2 **egg yolks**
(wings, necks, backs)	¾ **cup plain yogurt**
2 **stalks celery, sliced**	½ **head Bibb lettuce, coarsely**
1 **leek, sliced**	**chopped**
1 **large carrot, cubed**	

Bring water, salt, and chicken parts to boil in large saucepan; cover. Simmer 1 hour. Add celery, leek, carrot, and potatoes; simmer 20 minutes. Remove chicken. Cube meat and return to soup. Add peas; simmer about 8 minutes. Remove froth from surface of soup.

Lightly beat egg yolks and stir into yogurt.

Remove soup from heat; stir in yogurt mixture. Adjust seasoning. Garnish with lettuce and serve at once. Makes 6 servings.

Turkey and Chestnut Soup Leftover-Style

Carcass of 1 cooked turkey
3 to 4 tablespoons or more
 leftover chestnut stuffing
 (or 5 to 6 tablespoons
 canned chestnut puree)
2 onions, sliced
2 or 3 carrots, sliced
2 or 3 stalks celery, sliced
Several sprigs parsley
1 bay leaf

5 to 6 cups turkey stock or
 water
Salt and pepper
1 tablespoon butter
¾ tablespoon all-purpose
 flour
5 or 6 chestnuts
1 tablespoon parsley,
 chopped

Remove remaining chestnut stuffing from cold turkey; reserve. Remove turkey meat that can be used as garnish. Break up carcass; put into large pan with onions, carrots, celery, and herbs. Cover with water; simmer until well flavored. Avoid boiling hard—this makes stock cloudy. Strain.

Put chestnut stuffing into electric blender or food processor with cup of turkey stock; blend until smooth. Turn into pan. Add 4 cups stock, seasoning, and turkey meat. Cook together a few minutes. If the soup is too thin, blend butter and flour together to make paste; add to soup in small pieces. Stir until thickened. Bring to boil.

Serve hot with cooked chestnuts, fried in butter and broken into pieces. Sprinkle top with chopped parsley. Makes 4 to 6 servings.

Turkey-Vegetable Soup

1 small onion, chopped
2 tablespoons butter or
 margarine
2 cups water
2 chicken bouillon cubes
2 cups cooked turkey, diced
½ cup celery tops and pieces

1½ cups potatoes, diced
1 cup carrots, diced
2½ cups milk
2 tablespoons flour
1 teaspoon salt
⅛ teaspoon pepper

Cook onion in butter until tender. Add water, bouillon cubes, turkey, and vegetables; boil gently, covered, until vegetables are tender.

Stir a little milk into flour until mixture is smooth. Add remaining milk, salt, and pepper; add to soup. Simmer, stirring occasionally to prevent sticking, until soup is slightly thickened. Makes 6 servings.

Creamy Chicken Salad

Salads and Gravies

Chicken-Stuffed Apples

½ cup heavy cream, lightly
beaten
1¼ cups mayonnaise
Salt and pepper to taste
2 cups cooked white chicken
meat, finely diced
½ cup pineapple chunks,
drained

1 cup grapes, peeled and
seeded
2 stalks celery, chopped
4 large apples
1 teaspoon lemon rind,
grated
2 tablespoons slivered
almonds, lightly browned

Add cream to mayonnaise; season. Mix chicken with pineapple, grapes, and celery; mix with mayonnaise.

Polish apples; cut off top quarter of each. Scoop out flesh with grapefruit knife or spoon and remove cores. Dice remaining apple; add to mayonnaise.

Fill apples with chicken mayonnaise. Sprinkle tops with lemon rind and almonds. Makes 4 servings.

Avocado and Chicken Salad

3 **ripe avocado pears**	**Pinch of paprika**
2 **tablespoons orange juice**	**Salt to taste**
1 **cup cooked chicken, diced**	1 **tablespoon pimiento,**
1 **or 2 stalks celery, diced**	**chopped**
3 **oranges**	**Salad greens**
¼ **cup mayonnaise**	

Peel avocados, remove stones, and scoop out some flesh. Brush avocados with orange juice. Cut scooped-out flesh into small pieces; place in bowl with chicken and celery.

Peel and section 2 oranges; remove seeds and white pith. Cut into small pieces and add to chicken mixture.

Combine mayonnaise with paprika. Add salt; blend with chicken. Fill avocado halves; sprinkle with pimiento. Serve on bed of salad greens; garnish with sections of remaining orange. Makes 6 servings.

Waldorf Chicken Salad

Chicken Breasts with Celery Salad

4 chicken breasts	1 teaspoon prepared mustard
1 lemon	1 cup olive oil
Salt	¼ cup red-wine vinegar
Pepper	3 tablespoons Roquefort
Butter	cheese
6 stalks celery	
¼ cup walnuts, coarsely	Lettuce
chopped	Snipped chives

Vinaigrette
2 teaspoons salt
½ teaspoon freshly ground
   pepper

Place chicken breasts in a bowl with juice from 1 lemon. Add salt and pepper. Allow chicken to marinate while the salad is being made.

Cut celery into small pieces and chop walnuts into fairly large pieces. Combine Vinaigrette ingredients. Mash cheese into Vinaigrette or mix it in a blender or food processor. Blend with celery and nuts. Place leaves of lettuce on individual plates or a large serving plate.

Fry chicken breasts in butter. When they have become golden brown and are cooked through, cut them into slices and place them, warm, on lettuce leaves. Place salad on top of chicken, sprinkle with snipped chives, and decorate with watercress, if you have it on hand. Serve immediately while chicken is warm.

It is also tasty to serve cold chicken leftovers, which have been sprinkled with lemon juice, in this manner. Makes 4 servings.

Creamy Chicken Salad

2 cups cream of chicken soup	1 onion, grated
½ cup milk	2 tomatoes, skinned and chopped
2 level tablespoons gelatin	2 sticks celery, chopped
1 cup cold chicken	Salt and pepper
1 can sweetcorn, drained	

Put cream of chicken soup into a saucepan with milk and heat gently. Stir gelatin with 4 tablespoons hot water until dissolved. Add it to soup and stir well. Do not boil. Allow soup to cool.

Cut chicken into bite-sized pieces and stir it into soup. Add drained sweetcorn, onion, tomato, and celery. Taste and season if necessary.

Put salad into a 1-quart mold and chill until set. Unmold chicken salad onto a serving plate and serve with a green salad. Makes 4 to 6 servings.

Crisp Baked Chicken

Waldorf Chicken Salad

4 **dessert apples**	2 **sticks celery, chopped**
Juice of ½ lemon	1 **tablespoon walnuts,**
½ **cup mayonnaise**	**chopped**
Salt and pepper	**Lettuce leaves for serving**
1 **cup cooked chicken, diced**	

Peel, core, and dice apples. Mix apple with lemon juice to prevent it discoloring. Season mayonnaise with salt and pepper and put it in a bowl with diced apple, chicken, celery, and walnuts. Mix lightly.

Arrange lettuce on a serving plate. Place prepared salad in the middle and serve. Makes 4 servings.

Curried Chicken Salad

3 tablespoons instant minced onion	1 (1-pound, 4-ounce) can pineapple chunks, drained
3 tablespoons water	½ cup nuts, coarsely chopped
2 tablespoons butter	⅓ cup golden raisins
1¼ teaspoons curry powder	1 red apple, cored and sliced
⅓ cup mayonnaise	Lettuce
1 tablespoon lemon juice	2 tablespoons shredded coconut
½ teaspoon salt	
Dash of cayenne pepper	
3 cups cooked chicken, diced	

Combine onion and water in small bowl; let stand 10 minutes.

Melt butter in small skillet over medium heat; stir in onion and curry powder. Sauté, stirring constantly, 3 to 5 minutes; cool. Combine curry mixture with mayonnaise, lemon juice, salt, and cayenne; blend thoroughly.

Combine chicken, pineapple, nuts, raisins, and apple in large bowl. Add curry dressing; toss gently until mixed. Line salad bowl with lettuce. Add salad; sprinkle with coconut. Makes 6 servings.

Sorrento Salad

3 cups cooked chicken, diced	⅔ cup blue-cheese dressing
1 cup celery, chopped	2 cups orange sections
¼ cup red sweet pepper, chopped (optional)	2 cups grapefruit sections
½ teaspoon salt	½ cup avocado, diced
½ teaspoon pepper	1 avocado, cut into wedges
	Orange or grapefruit juice
	Salad greens

Combine chicken, celery, and red pepper in bowl; sprinkle with salt and pepper. Add blue-cheese dressing; toss to mix well. Chill thoroughly.

Dice enough orange and grapefruit sections to make 1/2 cup each; add to chicken mixture.

Coat diced avocado and avocado wedges with orange juice. Add diced avocado to chicken mixture.

Line large salad bowl with salad greens; spoon salad into bowl. Arrange remaining orange and grapefruit sections and avocado wedges around salad. Serve with additional blue-cheese dressing. Makes 6 servings.

Hawaiian Barbecued Chicken

Turkey, Celery, Grape, and Nut Salad

2 cups turkey, chopped	**Juice of ½ lemon**
½ cup grapes	**Grated rind of ½ orange**
½ cup celery, sliced	**1 cup mayonnaise**
3 to 4 tablespoons almonds	**Lettuce or endive leaves**

Chop turkey into medium-sized pieces. Dip grapes into boiling, then cold, water; peel. Slice celery. Dip almonds in boiling water; remove skins. Brown halved nuts in moderate oven 2 minutes.

Add lemon juice and orange rind to mayonnaise. Mix turkey and other ingredients into mayonnaise. Arrange on lettuce. Makes 4 servings.

Gravy

1 to 2 tablespoons flour	**1 cup liquid**
1 to 2 tablespoons fat or drippings	

For thin gravy use 1 tablespoon each flour and fat or drippings to each cup of liquid. For medium gravy use 2 tablespoons flour and 1 or 2 tablespoons fat or drippings, as desired. If drippings are scant, add bouillon cube or a little meat extract to liquid.

Method 1 (Use with fat or with drippings containing only fat and browned crusty bits.) Measure fat or drippings. Stir flour into fat; brown over low heat. Add liquid slowly, stirring constantly. Cook until thickened; stirring occasionally. Season to taste. Makes 1 cup.

Method 2 (Use with fat or drippings containing considerable amount of liquid.) Measure drippings; if necessary add water to make desired amount of liquid. Heat.

Combine flour with equal amount cold water by stirring or shaking until smooth; stir slowly into hot liquid. Cook until thickened, stir occasionally. Season to taste. Makes 1 cup.

Cheesy Oven-Fried Chicken

Giblet Gravy

**4 to 6 tablespoons flour, or 2
  to 3 tablespoons
  cornstarch
Turkey giblets, finely minced
3 to 4½ cups turkey broth,
  strained**

**Sage
Salt and pepper
Worcestershire sauce**

Remove turkey from pan. Skim off excess fat; leave drippings. Sprinkle flour or cornstarch into pan; stir to incorporate brown bits. Stir in finely minced giblets from broth. Gradually add strained turkey broth. Add sage, salt, pepper, and Worcestershire sauce to taste. Bring to boil, stirring until thickened and well blended. Makes about 5 cups.

Chicken Dishes

Crisp Baked Chicken

1   (3-pound) chicken
Salt and pepper
4   tablespoons margarine
2   tablespoons flour
2   level teaspoons curry
    powder

1   cup milk
2   tablespoons potato chips,
    crushed
2   tablespoons cheese, grated

Cut chicken into 4 portions; wipe with a damp cloth and season with salt and pepper. Place chicken in an ovenproof dish, dot with half the margarine, and cook in a 400°F oven for 40 minutes.

Meanwhile, melt remaining margarine in a saucepan; stir in flour and curry powder. Cook gently for 2 minutes.

Stir in milk gradually; then bring to a boil, stirring, until sauce is smooth and thickened. Season to taste. Pour sauce over chicken.

Mix crushed chips and cheese together and sprinkle on top of sauce. Return to oven or place under a hot grill until beginning to brown. Makes 4 servings.

Cinnamon Orange Chicken

Chicken and Artichoke Hearts

1	large onion	¾	cup sour cream
4	boned chicken breasts	1	cup white wine
Salt		1	can artichoke hearts
1	stick butter	5	slices crisp bacon
2½	teaspoons paprika		(crumbled)
4	tablespoons flour	**Slivered almonds**	
½	cup chicken stock	**Salt to taste**	

Chop onion finely. Skin chicken; sprinkle with salt.

Heat butter in frying pan; brown chicken. Remove chicken from pan. Sauté onion and paprika in remaining butter; remove pan from heat. Stir in flour; return to heat. Gradually add stock; stir until mixture boils and thickens. Add sour cream and wine; simmer lightly. Makes 4 servings.

Hawaiian Barbecued Chicken

1	(3-pound) chicken	1	level teaspoon curry powder
1	red pepper	1	cup tomato juice
1	green pepper	½	level teaspoon each ground ginger, cayenne, pepper, and salt
1	clove garlic, crushed		
1	small onion, grated		
2	level teaspoons brown sugar	1	tablespoon lemon juice

Cut all meat from chicken and cut into bite-sized pieces. Wash peppers, remove all seeds and membranes, and cut into squares. Thread chicken and peppers alternately onto 4 skewers. Place kebabs in a shallow bowl.

Mix all remaining ingredients in a bowl and whisk thoroughly together. Pour marinade over kebabs and leave in a cool place for up to 2 hours, turning occasionally.

Grill kebabs for 10 to 20 minutes, or until chicken is cooked. Baste occasionally with marinade. Makes 4 servings.

Spicy Barbecued Chicken

6	tablespoons oil	1	teaspoon French mustard
1	onion, finely chopped	1	teaspoon paprika
1	clove garlic, crushed		Juice and grated rind of ½ lemon
1	medium can tomatoes (or 3 to 4 tablespoons tomato puree)	2	teaspoons brown sugar
1	tablespoon tomato catsup	1	tablespoon parsley, finely chopped
1	tablespoon chutney	1	teaspoon mixed powdered thyme, nutmeg, and bay leaf
1	tablespoon vinegar		
½	cup stock (or water)		
1	tablespoon Worcestershire sauce	4	large chicken quarters or halves

Prepare barbecue sauce: Heat oil; cook onion and garlic 5 minutes. Add sieved tomatoes or puree and all other ingredients, except chicken. Cook 20 to 30 minutes; season to taste. Strain; let cool.

With sharp knife, make small cuts in chicken pieces. Spoon cold barbecue sauce over; let stand at least 1/2 hour.

Heat charcoal grill or broiler. Place chicken pieces on hot grill; turn every 5 or 6 minutes, basting frequently with barbecue sauce. Allow 30 to 45 minutes to barbecue quarters, depending on heat of grill and thickness of chicken. Test with skewer; if juice from chicken runs clear, chicken is done.

Heat remaining sauce; serve. Makes 4 servings.

Chicken in Cider and Mustard

Chicken with Biscuit Topping

Filling

2 tablespoons vegetable oil
1 small onion, peeled and chopped
½ green pepper, finely chopped
⅔ cup mushrooms, sliced
2 tablespoons cornstarch
1½ cups milk
1½ to 2 cups cooked chicken, cut into cubes

Salt and pepper

Biscuits

2 cups flour
1 teaspoon salt
2½ teaspoons baking powder
⅓ cup butter or margarine
About ⅔ cup milk

Heat oil in skillet. Add onion, green pepper, and mushrooms; sauté a few minutes. Add cornstarch; cook 1 minute, stirring all the time. Add milk gradually; stir until boiling. Add chicken and seasoning. Turn into deep 8- or 9-inch pie plate.

To make biscuits, sift flour, salt, and baking powder. Cut in butter with pastry blender until mixture looks like coarse bread crumbs. Using fork, stir in enough milk to make soft but not sticky dough. Knead lightly on floured board; roll about 1/2 inch thick. Cut into 1-1/2 inch rounds with cookie cutter. Place rounds on top of chicken mixture; brush with milk. Bake at 450°F 10 to 15 minutes. Makes 4 servings.

Brunswick Stew

1 stewing or roasting chicken, about 3 to 4 pounds
1 teaspoon salt
3 potatoes, sliced
1 large onion, sliced
1 cup green lima beans
1 cup canned tomatoes (or 5 or 6 sliced fresh tomatoes)
1 tablespoon sugar
1 cup kernel corn
1 tablespoon catsup or Worcestershire sauce (optional)
4 tablespoons butter

Cut chicken into pieces; put in casserole with enough boiling water to cover. Add salt and simmer about 45 minutes. Add potatoes, onion, lima beans, tomatoes, and sugar; cook 45 minutes. Beans and potatoes should be tender.

Remove chicken bones. Add corn; cook 10 minutes. Season to taste. Add catsup and butter; stir well. Makes 4 to 6 servings.

Chicken Country-Style

Cheesy Oven-Fried Chicken

1	(2½-pound) chicken
1	level tablespoon plain flour
	Salt and pepper
½	level teaspoon dry mustard
1	egg, beaten
¼	cup soft white bread crumbs
¼	cup Cheddar cheese, grated
4	tablespoons margarine

Cut chicken into 4 portions and wipe with a damp cloth. Season flour with salt, pepper, and mustard. Coat chicken in flour, then in beaten egg, and finally in the bread crumbs and cheese, mixed together.

Place in a roasting pan and dot with small pieces of margarine. Cook in 400°F oven for about 40 minutes or until golden and tender. Makes 4 servings.

Chicken Cordon Bleu

4 single boneless chicken breasts	½ teaspoon salt
4 tablespoons cooked ham, chopped	⅛ teaspoon white pepper
4 tablespoons Swiss cheese, grated	3 to 4 tablespoons seasoned flour
1 small clove garlic, crushed	1 large egg
1 to 2 tablespoons white wine	¼ cup oil
	6 to 8 tablespoons dried white bread crumbs
	4 to 5 tablespoons butter

Place chicken breasts skin-side-down. With sharp knife, cut a shallow slit down center of each without cutting through to skin. Cut shallow pockets on either side of these slits.

Mix ham and cheese with garlic and a little white wine to moisten. Season well. Fill pockets in chicken breasts; seal slit with small finger-shaped fillet attached to each breast. Put in refrigerator to chill 30 minutes. Coat well in seasoned flour. Brush carefully with egg beaten with 1 teaspoon oil; roll in bread crumbs.

Heat oil; add butter. When foaming, fry chicken breasts until tender, golden brown, and crisp all over. Drain on paper towel. Makes 4 servings.

Cinnamon Orange Chicken

1 (3-pound) chicken	4 tablespoons margarine
2 tablespoons flour	½ cup chicken stock or water and chicken stock cube
Salt and pepper	
1 level teaspoon ground cinnamon	2 oranges
	Freshly boiled rice for serving

Cut chicken into 4 portions and wipe with a damp cloth. Mix flour, salt, pepper, and cinnamon together and coat the chicken portions.

Heat margarine in a large frying pan and fry chicken until tender and golden all over (about 20 minutes). Remove chicken and drain on paper towels. Keep hot.

Pour off fat from pan. Add chicken stock and the finely grated rind and juice from 1 orange. Bring to a boil, stirring.

Arrange chicken on a bed of boiled rice and pour sauce over the top. Carefully peel remaining orange, removing all skin and pith; slice thinly. Arrange orange slices on chicken. Serve with rice. Makes 4 servings.

Creole Chicken

Chicken in Cider and Mustard

- 1 spring chicken
- ½ tablespoon margarine
- 1 large onion, peeled and thinly sliced
- ½ to 1 teaspoon salt
- ½ teaspoon black pepper
- ⅔ cup apple cider
- 1 tablespoon light French mustard
- ½ teaspoon dried, or 2 sprigs fresh, thyme
- ⅔ cup light cream

Divide chicken into 6 to 8 pieces. Brown chicken on all sides in margarine. Add sliced onion, salt, pepper, and cider. Mix mustard and thyme with light cream and pour it into the pot.

Mix thoroughly and let chicken simmer for 30 to 35 minutes. Serve with chopped parsley, boiled potatoes, and tender boiled carrots. Makes 4 servings.

Chicken Cordon Gold

12 **boneless chicken-breast halves**	12 **thin slices ham**
¾ **cup flour**	¼ **cup melted butter**
2 **teaspoons salt**	1 **cup plus 2 tablespoons Galliano liqueur**
½ **teaspoon white pepper**	⅓ **cup butter**
1 **package Boursin herb cheese**	½ **pound mushrooms, sliced**
	1 **bunch parsley**

Dredge chicken in flour mixed with salt and pepper. Place 2 tablespoons cheese and a slice of ham on each breast. Roll up each breast; secure with toothpicks. Close ends with toothpicks. Brown lightly in butter. Pour in 1 cup Galliano; cover skillet. Simmer until tender, about 30 minutes.

Heat 1/3 cup butter and 2 tablespoons Galliano in second skillet. Add mushrooms and sauté until crisp. Add parsley and sauté 3 minutes. Combine mixture with chicken 5 minutes before serving. Remove toothpicks before serving. Makes 6 servings.

Chicken Country-Style

1 **small cooked chicken**	½ **cup chicken stock or water and chicken stock cube**
6 **tablespoons margarine**	2 **tablespoons flour**
2 **carrots, diced**	1 **cup milk**
1 **small turnip, diced**	4 **tablespoons Cheddar cheese, grated**
1 **leek, sliced**	¼ **teaspoon dry mustard**
1 **onion, chopped**	**Parsley for garnish**
2 **sticks celery, sliced**	
Salt and pepper	
1 **level teaspoon sugar**	

Cut chicken into pieces and remove meat from bones. Heat 4 tablespoons of margarine in a saucepan. Add prepared vegetables, salt, pepper, and sugar. Fry very gently, stirring occasionally, for 10 minutes. Add chicken stock, cover pan, and bring to a boil. Then simmer gently for 20 minutes.

Melt remaining margarine in a saucepan; stir in flour. Cook, stirring, for 2 minutes. Add milk gradually, then bring to a boil, stirring until sauce is thickened and smooth. Stir grated cheese and mustard into sauce.

Put drained vegetables in an ovenproof dish, arrange chicken on top, and pour sauce over top. Bake in 400°F oven for 20 minutes. Serve garnished with parsley. Makes 4 servings.

Deviled Chicken Casserole

Chicken Curry

1 **frying chicken, cut into serving pieces**	2 **cups chicken broth**
2 **tablespoons vegetable oil**	**Salt and pepper to taste**
2 **tablespoons butter or margarine**	2 **teaspoons curry powder**
2 **cups cooked barley**	1 **teaspoon marjoram**
1 **medium onion, minced**	1 **cup plain yogurt**
	1 **tomato, peeled, seeded, cut into bite-sized pieces**

Brown chicken in oil and butter in large skillet. Remove chicken from pan; place on bed of barley in Dutch oven or flameproof casserole.

In same skillet, cook onion in remaining oil and butter until transparent. Remove; place on top of chicken. Pour 1-1/2 cups broth over chicken and barley. Sprinkle with salt, pepper, curry powder, and marjoram. Cover; cook over low heat 30 minutes. Remove cover. Add yogurt, tomato, and 1/2 cup broth, if needed. Cook, uncovered, 20 to 30 minutes, until chicken is tender. Makes 4 to 6 servings.

Creole Chicken

1 **(2½-pound) chicken**	2 **(14-ounce) cans crushed**
6 to 7 **slices of bacon**	**tomatoes**
⅓ **cup flour**	2 **teaspoons thyme**
1 **tablespoon olive oil**	1 **teaspoon black pepper**
¾ **cup onion, sliced**	¼ **teaspoon cayenne pepper**
1 **clove garlic, chopped**	1 **bay leaf**
2 to 3 **celery stalks**	**Juice from ½ lemon**
1 **green pepper, shredded**	

Divide chicken into 8 pieces. Fry bacon slices until brown and crispy in a stew pot. Take them out and let them drain on a paper towel.

Dredge chicken pieces in flour and fry them in bacon fat so that they become golden brown all over. Take them out of the pot. Pour olive oil into pot and add onion and garlic. After about 5 minutes, add celery and green pepper.

After another 3 minutes, add canned tomatoes and rest of the spices. Let mixture come to a boil. Place chicken pieces on vegetable mixture, cover, and let simmer for 30 minutes. Add a little water if mixture becomes too dry.

Just before serving, add lemon juice. Then sprinkle with bacon slices, which also can be slightly crumbled. Serve with rice. Makes 4 servings.

Chicken Croquettes

4 **cups cooked chicken, put through meat grinder**	**Generous dash of freshly ground pepper**
1 **cup celery, chopped**	1 **egg, beaten with 1 tablespoon milk**
1 **tablespoon onion, grated**	1 **cup cracker meal**
4 **tablespoons butter**	**Oil for deep frying**
4 **tablespoons flour**	2 **cans cream of mushroom soup for quick sauce**
1 **cup milk**	
1 **teaspoon salt**	

Mix chicken and celery in large bowl; set aside.

Sauté onion in butter in small saucepan until onion is transparent. Blend flour. Add milk; heat, stirring constantly. When slightly thickened, add salt and pepper; simmer just 3 minutes. Add sauce to chicken and celery and chill several hours.

Shape chicken into rolls about 3 inches long. Dip into egg; roll in cracker meal. Place croquettes on waxed-paper-lined baking sheet; chill in refrigerator at least 3 hours.

Chicken Drumsticks with Rice

Fry croquettes in deep fat, a few at a time, until brown on all sides; drain on paper towels. Can be kept warm in very low (250°F) oven until ready to serve.

For a quick sauce with croquettes, heat cream of mushroom soup over low heat; stir until piping hot. If you prefer thinner sauce, add milk by 1/4 cups; stir until desired consistency is reached. Makes 4 to 6 servings.

Deviled Chicken Casserole

1 **(3-pound) chicken**	2 **tablespoons vinegar**
1 **tablespoon oil**	1 **level teaspoon French**
1 **small onion, finely**	**mustard**
chopped	1 **cup tomato juice**
1 **clove garlic, crushed**	½ **cup chicken stock or water**
1 **stick celery, chopped**	**and chicken stock cube**
1 **level tablespoon brown**	**Salt and pepper**
sugar	
2 **tablespoons Worcestershire**	
sauce	

Cut chicken into pieces. Heat oil in a frying pan and fry chicken until brown all over. Drain well and put into an ovenproof casserole.

Mix all remaining ingredients together in a bowl and pour them over chicken. Cover casserole and cook in a 325°F oven for 1 to 1-1/4 hours or until the chicken is tender. Makes 4 to 6 servings.

Chicken Drumsticks with Rice

12 **chicken drumsticks**	**Salt and pepper**
2 **eggs, beaten**	2 **red peppers, chopped**
½ **cup bread crumbs**	1 **cup frozen peas**
2 **level teaspoons mixed**	1 **cup frozen sweetcorn**
dried herbs	6 **tomatoes, skinned and**
Oil for deep-frying	**chopped**
1½ **cups long-grain rice**	**Sprigs of watercress**

Coat drumsticks with beaten egg. Mix bread crumbs and mixed herbs together. Press them onto drumsticks. Fill a deep frying pan 1/3 to 1/2 full of oil and heat. When hot add drumsticks, 3 at a time; fry for 15 to 20 minutes. Drain on absorbent kitchen paper and leave to cool.

Cook rice in a large saucepan of boiling salted water for 12 to 15 minutes or until tender. Drain in a sieve, then rinse under cold running water. Cook chopped red pepper in boiling water for 3 minutes; rinse with cold water and stir into rice. Cook peas and sweetcorn together in boiling salted water for 5 minutes. Drain; then rinse with cold water and add to rice with chopped tomatoes. Toss well together. Add salt and pepper to taste.

Serve piled on 2 plates in a pyramid shape. Arrange the cooled drumsticks on the rice. Garnish with sprigs of watercress. Makes 12 servings.

Breast of Chicken Florentine

½   cup flour
1   teaspoon salt
⅛   teaspoon white pepper
6   chicken breasts, boned
    and skinned
2   eggs, beaten
½   cup Parmesan cheese
¾   cup bread crumbs

¾   cup butter
1   pound mushrooms, sliced
Chopped parsley
4   packages frozen leaf
    spinach
2   tablespoons lemon juice
Dash of nutmeg

Mix flour, salt, and pepper; dredge chicken with seasoned flour. Dip in egg; coat with cheese and bread crumbs. Refrigerate at least 1 hour.

Heat 1/2 cup butter in large skillet; brown chicken on each side. Lower heat; cover. Simmer 25 minutes. Remove chicken from skillet.

Add mushrooms and parsley to drippings; stir over heat 3 minutes.

Cook spinach until tender, then drain well. Season with 1/4 cup butter, lemon juice, salt, pepper, and nutmeg.

Serve chicken on bed of spinach; top with mushrooms. (Chicken can be cooked in advance and heated in hot oven.) Makes 6 servings.

Chicken Italian-Style

1   (3-pound) chicken
Salt and pepper
3   tablespoons olive oil
1   onion, sliced
2   sticks celery, chopped
1   cup or 2 medium-sized
    tomatoes, skinned and
    chopped

1   cup chicken stock or water
    and chicken stock cube
½   teaspoon each dried basil
    and marjoram
½   pound spaghetti
Chopped parsley for garnish

Chop chicken into 4 portions and wipe with a damp cloth. Season with salt and pepper. Heat oil in a large frying pan and fry chicken until golden. Remove from pan. Add onion and celery to oil and fry for a few minutes. Add tomatoes, then the stock and herbs. Bring to a boil and simmer for 5 minutes. Return chicken to pan; cover and continue cooking for 30 minutes or until chicken is tender.

Meanwhile, cook spaghetti in a large pan of boiling salted water for about 10 minutes or until tender. Drain spaghetti well, then arrange it on a serving plate. Top with chicken and sauce. Serve garnished with chopped parsley. Makes 4 servings.

Chicken à la King

Chicken Kampama

1	(3-pound) chicken, cut up	½	of 6-ounce can tomato paste
2	tablespoons butter		
2	tablespoons olive oil	2	sticks cinnamon
2	medium onions, chopped	¼	teaspoon ground allspice
2	cloves garlic, minced	½	teaspoon sugar
1	cup canned tomatoes	¼	cup red wine

In large skillet, brown chicken on all sides in butter and olive oil; remove from pan.

Brown onions and garlic. Add tomatoes, tomato paste, seasonings, and wine; bring to boil. Add chicken. Reduce heat to simmer; cook 1 to 1-1/2 hours or until tender. Makes 4 or 5 servings.

Chicken à la King

1 cup cold cooked chicken	1 cup long-grain rice
6 tablespoons margarine	Salt
1 onion, finely chopped	1 level tablespoon chopped
½ cup mushrooms, chopped	parsley, and extra for
1 green pepper, chopped	garnish
1 (10½-ounce) can	
condensed chicken or	
mushroom soup	

Cut chicken into bite-sized pieces. Melt 4 tablespoons margarine in a frying pan and fry onion until softened. Add mushrooms and pepper and cook, stirring, for 2 to 3 minutes. Stir in soup and chicken. Bring to a boil; simmer very gently for 10 to 15 minutes.

Meanwhile, cook rice in a large saucepan with plenty of boiling salted water for 10 to 15 minutes. Drain well, then stir in parsley and remaining margarine. Arrange rice on a serving plate and pile chicken mixture on top. Garnish with chopped parsley. Makes 4 servings.

Chicken with Green Peppers and Bamboo Shoots in Oyster Sauce

Sauce	**Chicken-Vegetable Mixture**
1 small onion, sliced	1 tablespoon vegetable oil
1 tablespoon soy sauce	1 large green pepper, cut
2 tablespoons oyster sauce	into ¾-inch cubes
(found in Oriental food	¼ cup bamboo shoots, sliced
stores and some	¼ pound small whole
supermarkets)	mushrooms
¾ cup chicken broth	2 whole chicken breasts,
1 teaspoon brown sugar	split, skinned, boned, and
1 teaspoon gingerroot,	cut into pieces
freshly grated	½ cucumber, peeled, and cut
1 tablespoon cornstarch in 2	into chunks
tablespoons water	

To make sauce, simmer all sauce ingredients together 8 to 10 minutes; stir occasionally.

Meanwhile, heat oil in frying pan (or wok); stir-fry green pepper 3 minutes. Remove; reserve. Stir-fry bamboo shoots and mushrooms 2 to 3 minutes; reserve with green pepper. Add chicken to pan; stir-fry 3 to 4 minutes or until done. Return vegetables to pan with chicken. Add cucumber. Immediately add oyster sauce; heat through. Serve with rice. Makes 4 servings.

Lemon and Garlic-Filled Chicken Breasts

Lemon and Garlic-Filled Chicken Breasts

8 chicken breasts	2 tablespoons parsley, finely
Salt	chopped
Pepper	Flour
7 tablespoons butter, at room	1 egg, beaten
temperature	Bread crumbs
3 cloves garlic, crushed	Oil
Juice of 1 lemon	

Remove bones and pound breasts until quite thin. Salt and pepper them slightly. Mix butter with garlic, lemon juice, parsley, salt, and pepper. Spread butter mixture on chicken breasts, fold in the edges, and roll them together. Fasten with a toothpick.

First roll breasts in flour, then dip them in a beaten egg. Finally roll in bread crumbs. Fry them rather slowly in hot oil until they are golden brown and cooked through.

Serve with peeled, seeded cucumbers, which have simmered slightly in the rest of the butter, and rice. Makes 4 servings.

Marinated Chicken

1 chicken, about 2½ pounds	**Cucumber Salad**
	2 cups yogurt
Marinade	½ to ¾ cucumber
2 cups yogurt	¼ cup chives, finely snipped
1 onion, peeled and sliced	1 teaspoon salt
2 teaspoons curry	Black pepper
1 teaspoon ginger	
2 teaspoons paprika	
1 teaspoon caraway	
1 to 2 cloves garlic, crushed	

Divide chicken in half. Mix all marinade ingredients together. Place chicken halves in a deep plate. Cover with marinade; refrigerate for 6 to 8 hours. Turn chicken several times while it is marinating.

Preheat oven to 350°F. Place chicken halves in an ovenproof dish. Pour marinade over chicken and brush chicken well. Bake for about 45 minutes. Brush chicken occasionally with the marinade while it is baking.

When making cucumber salad, allow yogurt to drain through a coffee filter for about 15 minutes. Thinly slice cucumber. (it is easiest to do this with a cheese slicer). Mix with yogurt. Add chives; season with salt and pepper. Serve with brown rice. Makes 4 servings.

Marinated Chicken

Mediterranean Chicken

1 tablespoon butter or margarine	2 (10½-ounce) cans condensed cream of mushroom soup
1 tablespoon onion, finely chopped	½ teaspoon oregano
½ cup celery, chopped	White pepper to taste
1 (10-ounce) package frozen French-style green beans	⅔ cup cashew or roasted peanut halves
1 tablespoon pimiento, chopped	1 tablespoon minced parsley (optional)
2 cups cooked chicken, diced	

Melt butter in 2- or 3-quart saucepan. Add onion, celery, and beans. Cover; simmer over low heat about 15 minutes, stirring occasionally, until beans are tender. Add pimiento, chicken, soup, and seasonings. Cook 10 minutes to blend flavors; stir as needed to prevent sticking. Stir in nuts. Sprinkle with parsley before serving. Makes 6 servings.

Chicken Maryland

1	(2- to 2½-pound) chicken	4	tablespoons margarine
2	tablespoons flour	¼	cup self-rising flour
Salt and pepper		1	egg
1	egg, beaten	6	tablespoons water
Soft white bread crumbs		1	cup sweetcorn (canned or
Oil for deep-frying			frozen)
2	bananas		

Cut chicken into 4 serving portions. Mix flour, salt, and pepper together. Coat chicken in the flour, then in beaten egg, and finally in bread crumbs. Press coating on firmly. Heat oil for deep-frying. Fry chicken for 20 to 30 minutes or until cooked. The temperature may be reduced slightly if coating becomes overbrowned.

Meanwhile, prepare bananas by cutting them in half and frying in margarine for 2 to 3 minutes.

Make sweetcorn fritters: Sift flour into a bowl with a pinch of salt. Make a well in the center and add the egg. Mix in with a wooden spoon, then gradually add water. Beat until smooth. Stir in sweetcorn. Fry tablespoonfuls of the mixture in margarine until browned, turning once.

Drain cooked bananas, fritters, and chicken on absorbent kitchen paper and keep hot until needed. Makes 4 servings.

Chicken in Mint Sauce

1	(4-pound) chicken	4	tablespoons margarine
1	onion	4	tablespoons flour
6	cloves	2	level tablespoons chopped
6	peppercorns		fresh mint or 2 level
½	lemon		teaspoons dried mint
1	bay leaf	Salt and pepper	
1	cup milk		

Prepare chicken. Wipe inside with a clean damp cloth. Place it in a large saucepan with enough water almost to cover. Peel onion and stick cloves into it; add to saucepan with the peppercorns, lemon, and bay leaf. Bring to a boil; cover pan, and simmer gently for 1-1/4 to 1-1/2 hours or until tender. Keep hot.

Measure 1 cup of cooking liquid and mix it with milk. Melt margarine in a saucepan; add flour and cook, stirring, for 3 minutes. Add liquid gradually, stirring until sauce is thickened and smooth. Cook for 2 minutes. Stir in mint; taste and adjust seasoning.

Cut chicken into serving pieces and place on a heated dish. Pour sauce over the top and serve as soon as possible. Makes 6 servings.

Chicken Maryland

Mustard Chicken

1 (3-pound) chicken	1 teaspoon vinegar
Salt and pepper	2 thin slices bread
6 tablespoons margarine	Oil for frying
2 tablespoons flour	Parsley for garnish
1 cup milk	
2 level teaspoons dry mustard	

Cut chicken into 4 serving portions. Wipe with a frying pan and fry chicken until tender (about 20 minutes). Keep hot.

Stir flour into remaining fat and cook, stirring, for 2 to 3 minutes. Gradually blend in the milk, mustard, and salt and pepper to taste. Bring to a boil, stirring; simmer until smooth and thickened. Stir in vinegar.

Cut triangular shapes from the bread and fry them in oil until golden; drain. Arrange chicken in a serving dish, pour sauce over top, and garnish with fried bread triangles and sprigs of parsley. Makes 4 servings.

Chicken Normandy

1 **chicken, about 3½ pounds**	2 **tablespoons flour**
Salt and pepper	1½ **cups chicken bouillon or**
4 **tablespoons oil**	**water**
1 **onion, peeled and sliced**	**Pinch of thyme**
2 **stalks celery, sliced**	**Pinch of marjoram**
2 **large apples, peeled, cored**	2 **tablespoons grated cheese**
and sliced	**Boiled rice**

Cut chicken into small pieces; season with salt and pepper. Heat 3 tablespoons oil in pan. Add pieces of chicken (a few at a time); brown well. Remove pieces as they are browned.

Put onion, celery, and apples into remaining oil; cook until onion is tender. Add 1 tablespoon oil. Stir in flour; mix well. Gradually add bouillon; stir until boiling. Return chicken to sauce. Add thyme, marjoram, and a little seasoning. Cover; simmer until chicken is tender. Adjust the seasoning to taste. Stir in cheese.

To serve, put some hot cooked rice onto large platter; arrange pieces of chicken on top. Pour sauce over. Serve excess sauce separately. Makes 6 servings.

Oregano Grilled Chicken

3 **pounds fryer-chicken**	½ **teaspoon salt**
pieces	1 **teaspoon crumbled dried**
1 **large freezer bag**	**oregano**
½ **cup olive oil**	½ **teaspoon freshly ground**
¼ **cup lemon juice**	**pepper**
2 **cloves garlic, minced**	2 **tablespoons butter, melted**

The day before cooking, wash chicken; pat dry. Place in freezer bag. Combine oil, lemon juice, garlic, salt, oregano, and pepper; pour over chicken. Tie bag shut; turn bag several times to coat chicken with marinade. Refrigerate 24 hours, turning bag occasionally.

Remove chicken from bag; reserve marinade. Grill 5 inches from white-hot charcoal 30 minutes; turn once. Brush frequently with marinade combined with butter. Makes 4 or 5 servings

Variation: Substitute 1 (3-pound) roasting chicken for chicken parts; marinate in same manner. Drain chicken; reserve marinade. Mount on rotisserie spit and cook 1-1/2 hours on indoor unit or over charcoal. Baste frequently with marinade mixed with butter.

Chicken and Orange Kebabs

3 **oranges**	16 **small mushrooms**
4 **strips bacon**	1 **generous cup cold cooked**
6 **tablespoons margarine**	**chicken**

Peel 2 of the oranges, removing all pith and skin. Cut oranges into segments. Cut bacon into 1-inch squares and fry it. Remove bacon; add 2 tablespoons margarine, then fry mushrooms gently in bacon fat and margarine. Cut chicken into 1-inch pieces. Thread bacon, chicken, orange segments, and mushrooms onto 4 long skewers.

Squeeze juice from remaining orange. Heat juice in a small saucepan with remaining margarine. Brush kebabs with the mixture and cook under a hot broiler or on a grill until lightly browned all over, basting occasionally. Serve as soon as possible. Makes 4 servings.

Chicken in Mint Sauce

Mustard Chicken

Easy Paella

¼ **pound bacon**
½ **onion, chopped**
1 **clove garlic**
1 **red or green pepper, cubed**
2 **cups chicken broth**
¼ **teaspoon saffron**
Salt
Pepper
1 **cup rice**
1 **broiled chicken, cut up into smaller pieces**

1 **can clam meats**
1 **(10-ounce) package frozen peas**
About 20 large shrimp with shells
Oil
Garlic powder
Lemon wedges

Cut bacon into smaller pieces and brown them in a pot together with the onion, garlic, and red or green pepper. Pour mixture over the broth, which has been flavored with the saffron; season with salt and pepper. Bring to a boil. Add rice and cover pot. Simmer for about 25 minutes.

Warm pieces of chicken in rice mixture; add clams and peas. Dip shrimp in a little oil that has been seasoned with garlic powder and salt. Sauté them quickly in a hot frying pan; then place them in and on top of the rice.

Garnish with wedges of lemon. Makes 4 to 6 servings.

Chicken Paprika

1	(3-pound) chicken	1	large can tomatoes
¼	pound margarine	3	level tablespoons parsley, chopped
2	onions, chopped	½	cup mushrooms
1	clove garlic, crushed	4	tablespoons flour
2	teaspoons prepared mustard		Salt and pepper
1	level tablespoon paprika pepper	1	cup sour cream

Cut chicken into 4 to 6 pieces. Heat 1/2 the margarine in a large saucepan; add onion and garlic and fry gently for about 5 minutes, until softened and golden. Blend mustard and paprika pepper with tomatoes in a bowl. Stir in parsley, mushrooms, and fried onion mixture.

Put flour onto a large plate and use it to coat chicken pieces. Add remaining margarine to saucepan, add the coated chicken pieces, and fry them until golden brown all over. Put chicken into a casserole and cover with the tomato mixture. Cover the casserole and cook in 350°F oven for 1 hour or until chicken is tender. Leave to cool and store in refrigerator or in a cold place overnight.

The next day, stir in sour cream and put in a moderate 350°F oven for 30 to 40 minutes. Makes 4 to 6 servings.

Chicken Parmesan with Mushroom Marsala Sauce

2 to 3 tablespoons olive oil
6 to 8 pats butter

1	cup seasoned bread crumbs	1	cup flour seasoned with salt and pepper
1	cup Parmesan cheese, freshly grated	2	eggs, beaten in medium-sized bowl
1	tablespoon Herbes d'Provence (or herbs of your choice)		**Mushroom Marsala Sauce**
6	single chicken breasts (deboned)	1	pound fresh mushrooms
		3	to 4 tablespoons butter
		⅓	cup Marsala wine (or to taste)

Pour oil in center of 12-inch frying pan. Place pats of butter around oil, heat slowly to cooking temperature.

Combine bread crumbs, cheese, and herbs on plate. Wash and pat dry chicken. Coat with seasoned flour; dip in eggs. Coat with bread-crumb mixture. Set aside on waxed paper or rack; repeat procedure for all pieces. Let stand in refrigerator 2 to 3 hours.

Place all pieces in frying pan at same time; fry to golden brown.

Make sauce: Clean mushrooms; sauté in butter. Add wine and stir until hot (do not bring to boil). Pour sauce over chicken just before serving. Makes 6 servings.

Chicken Pie with Herb Topping

4 strips bacon, chopped	Salt and pepper
¼ cup mushrooms, sliced	⅔ cup self-rising flour
½ cup cooked chicken, cut into bite-sized pieces	6 tablespoons margarine
2 carrots, cooked and sliced	2 level tablespoons parsley, chopped
1 cup chicken stock or water and chicken stock cube	Cold water to mix
1 level tablespoon cornstarch	

Fry bacon in a saucepan until the fat runs. Add mushrooms and fry until softened. Add chicken, carrots, and stock. Mix cornstarch with a little of the stock; then return it to the pan. Bring to a boil, stirring constantly, until thickened. Season with salt and pepper. Pour into a shallow, ovenproof dish.

Sift flour into a bowl and rub in the margarine until it resembles fine bread crumbs. Stir in the parsley and a pinch of salt, then enough cold water to make a soft dough. Roll out dough to fit the dish and place it on chicken mixture. Mark with a knife to make a diamond pattern. Bake in 400°F oven for 15 to 20 minutes or until well risen and golden. Makes 4 servings.

Chicken Pilaf

1 (2½-pound) chicken	⅔ cup long-grain rice
6 tablespoons margarine	1½ cups chicken stock or water and chicken stock cube
1 onion, chopped	
2 strips bacon, chopped	Salt and pepper
2 sticks celery, chopped	
1 red or green pepper, chopped, or 1 small package frozen peas	

Cut chicken into 4 serving portions; wipe with a damp cloth, then rub all over with 2 tablespoons of margarine. Cook chicken under a preheated broiler until cooked and golden (about 20 minutes).

Meanwhile, heat remaining margarine in a saucepan; add onion, bacon, celery, pepper or peas, and rice. Cook, stirring, until rice begins to brown. Add the stock and bring to a boil. Cover pan and simmer gently for about 20 minutes, or until all liquid is absorbed. Taste and adjust seasoning.

Put rice on a serving plate with the chicken on top. Makes 4 servings.

Chicken in Potato Nest

2 cups cooked mashed potatoes	**¼ cup heavy cream**
2 tablespoons butter or margarine	**1 small can (about 3 ounces) sliced mushrooms**
2 tablespoons flour	**2 cups cooked chicken, diced**
Salt to taste	**2 tablespoons Parmesan cheese, grated**
½ teaspoon pepper	
1 cup chicken broth	

Line buttered 8- or 9-inch pie plate with potatoes.

Melt butter in pan; stir in flour and seasonings. Add broth gradually; stir until boiling. Add cream and mushrooms; cook a few minutes.

Put chicken into pie plate. Pour sauce over; sprinkle with cheese. Bake in a preheated 400°F oven 25 to 30 minutes. Makes 4 servings.

Chicken and Orange Kebobs

Chicken-Rice Casserole

2½ to 3 pounds fryer-chicken parts	1½ cups chicken broth
5 tablespoons butter or margarine	1 bay leaf
4 tablespoons olive oil	½ teaspoon salt
2 tablespoons sherry	¼ teaspoon pepper
1 small onion, chopped	Pinch of saffron
1 green pepper, chopped	2 medium tomatoes, peeled and sliced
1 clove garlic, minced	2 tablespoons Parmesan cheese
1 cup raw long-grain rice	

Wash chicken; pat dry. Heat 4 tablespoons each butter and oil in large skillet over moderate heat. Brown chicken well on all sides. Pour sherry over chicken; remove chicken from pan.

Add onion, green pepper, and garlic to pan; sauté until golden. Add rice; sauté 2 minutes. Add chicken broth, bay leaf, salt, pepper, and saffron; bring to boil.

Grease 2-quart casserole. Pour in rice mixture; top with chicken. Cover casserole and bake at 350°F 45 minutes.

Sauté tomatoes in 1 tablespoon butter; place on chicken. Sprinkle with cheese; bake 15 minutes. Makes 4 servings.

Grilled Chicken with Pineapple

4 chicken legs with thigh	Salt
1 small can pineapple pieces	1 level teaspoon cornstarch
1 tablespoon lemon juice	Watercress for garnish
4 tablespoons margarine	

Cut chicken joints in half to make 8 smaller pieces. Drain syrup from can of pineapple and mix it with lemon juice. Place chicken in a shallow dish; pour over the pineapple juice and let sit for 1 hour. Drain; dry chicken with paper towels. Rub with margarine, sprinkle with salt, and broil for about 20 minutes or until cooked and golden all over.

Meanwhile, place pineapple juice and pieces in a small saucepan. Mix cornstarch with a little of the juice and add it to the pan. Bring to a boil and cook, stirring, until thickened and clear. Season with salt to taste.

Arrange chicken on a serving dish; pour the pineapple with the thickened juice over chicken. Garnish with watercress. Makes 4 servings.

Easy Paella

Deviled Roast Chicken

2	(3-pound) roasting chickens	1½	level teaspoons salt
¼	pound margarine	1	level teaspoon pepper
6	tablespoons vinegar	¼	level teaspoon cayenne pepper
2	cloves garlic, crushed (optional)	3	teaspoons Worcestershire sauce
3	level teaspoons dry mustard	3	teaspoons soy sauce
		1	level tablespoon sugar

Cut each chicken into 6 portions or ask your butcher to do it for you. Place chicken pieces in a large roasting pan and dot with margarine. Roast in a 375°F oven for 45 minutes or until tender and browned.

Meanwhile, put all the remaining ingredients in a saucepan and bring to a boil. Arrange the cooked chicken pieces on a serving plate and cover with sauce. Serve as soon as possible. Makes 12 servings.

Roast Chicken

1 (3-pound) chicken	Grated rind of 1 lemon
Salt and pepper	½ level teaspoon mixed dried
¼ cup soft white bread	herbs
crumbs	Beaten egg to bind
4 tablespoons margarine	1 tablespoon margarine
1 tablespoon parsley,	Parsley for garnish
chopped	

Prepare chicken. Wipe inside and out with a clean damp cloth; season inside with salt and pepper. Mix bread crumbs, margarine, parsley, lemon rind, mixed herbs, and salt and pepper together in a bowl. Add enough egg to make a soft mixture.

Put stuffing in under the neck flap of the chicken. Truss chicken and rub it outside with margarine. Place in a roasting pan and cook in a 375°F oven for 1-1/4, hours. Serve on a hot plate, garnished with parsley. Makes 4 to 6 servings.

Chicken Skewers

Skewer	*Marinade*
Pieces of chicken liver	1 tablespoon brown sugar
wrapped up in bacon slices	1 tablespoon orange juice
Small pieces of chicken	1 teaspoon lemon juice
Small onions	½ teaspoon ginger
Tomato wedges	⅔ cup oil
Pieces of pineapple	Salt
A couple of strips of green	Pepper
pepper	Pinch cayenne pepper

Alternate meat and vegetables on a skewer. Combine marinade ingredients and baste meat and vegetables. Grill over coals or broil in the oven for 6 to 7 minutes on each side.

Serve with rice, preferably cooked in broth with chopped onion and seasoned with saffron. Also serve small bowls with the rest of the marinade and with peanut butter sauce in them.

To make peanut butter sauce: Beat together 1-1/4 cups sour cream and 3 to 4 tablespoons chopped salted nuts. Spice with plenty of onion powder.

Chicken Paprika

Spicy Roast Chicken

1	cup plain yogurt	1	teaspoon cumin
3	cloves garlic, crushed	½	teaspoon cayenne pepper
2	teaspoons fresh ginger, grated	1	whole chicken (3 pounds)
⅓	cup lime juice		Lime wedges
1	tablespoon ground coriander	1	onion, sliced and steamed

Mix yogurt, garlic, ginger, lime juice, and spices. Rub chicken inside and out with mixture. Place in bowl; pour remaining marinade over. Cover and refrigerate 24 hours. Turn chicken at least once.

Remove chicken from marinade. Roast in preheated 375°F oven 1 hour or until done. Baste with marinade during cooking. Disjoint chicken; serve with lime wedges and onion slices. Makes 4 servings.

Stuffed Chicken-Breasts Athenian

4	**split chicken breasts, skinned and boned**
2	**tablespoons feta cheese, crumbled**
1	**tablespoon walnuts, chopped**
1	**tablespoon parsley, chopped**
¾	**cup flour**
½	**teaspoon salt**
¼	**teaspoon pepper**
1	**egg**
2	**tablespoons milk**
2	**tablespoons olive oil**
2	**tablespoons butter**

Kima Sauce

3	**tablespoons olive oil**
¼	**cup onion, chopped**
¼	**cup carrots, chopped**
¼	**cup celery, chopped**
1	**clove garlic, chopped**
1	**(8-ounce) can tomatoes, drained and chopped**
2	**tablespoons parsley, chopped**
¼	**cup white wine**
¼	**teaspoon sugar**
¼	**teaspoon oregano**

Cut small pocket in each chicken cutlet by making slit in each piece; do not cut all the way through cutlet.

Mix cheese, walnuts, and parsley. Put 1 tablespoon stuffing in each cutlet; seal edges by pressing together.

Mix flour, salt, and pepper. Dredge chicken in flour mixture. Mix egg and milk. Dip cutlets in egg mixture, then again in flour mixture; refrigerate until ready to cook.

Heat oil and butter in large, heavy skillet over medium heat until foam subsides. Cook cutlets over medium-high heat until brown. Turn cutlets; reduce heat. Cook until brown and cooked through. Do not cover; chicken will lose its crispness and cheese will begin to ooze out of cutlet.

Make sauce: Heat oil in small, heavy skillet. Cook onion, carrots, celery, and garlic until limp. Add tomatoes, parsley, wine, sugar, and oregano; simmer 20 minutes or until thick.

Serve chicken with rice pilaf; top with kima sauce. Makes 4 servings.

Chicken Stew

½	**cup pork drippings or other cooking fat**
1	**boiling fowl, jointed**
	Salt and pepper
	Flour
2	**large onions, peeled and sliced**

2 or 3	**tomatoes, peeled, and quartered**
6 to 8	**green olives (optional)**
2	**bay leaves**
¼	**teaspoon mixed herbs**
	Stock or water
1	**cup mushrooms, sliced**

Chicken Pie with Herb Topping

Heat fat in kettle. Coat chicken pieces with flour to which salt and pepper have been added; brown on all sides. Remove chicken from pan. Add onions and tomatoes; fry about 5 minutes. Add olives, bay leaves, and herbs. Sprinkle with 2 tablespoons flour and a little salt and pepper; mix well. Replace chicken and add enough stock or water to cover. Cover kettle and simmer very slowly 2 to 2-1/2 hours, until chicken is tender.

When chicken is nearly done, add mushrooms; remove bay leaves. Put chicken on large dish and arrange vegetables around it. Thicken stock with a little extra flour; adjust seasoning. Pour some over chicken; serve rest separately. Makes 6 to 8 servings.

Spring Chicken Casserole

1 (2½-pound) chicken	1 turnip, diced
¼ pound margarine	2 level tablespoons flour
2 strips bacon, chopped	1½ cups chicken stock
12 small onions, peeled	Salt and pepper
1 pound small carrots	1 bay leaf

Cut chicken into serving portions and remove skin. Heat margarine in an ovenproof casserole. Fry chicken until lightly browned; remove and drain. Fry bacon; add onions, carrots, and turnip. Cover pan and cook very gently for 10 minutes.

Sprinkle in flour and cook, stirring, for 2 to 3 minutes. Stir in the stock and salt and pepper to taste. Bring to a boil, stirring all the time. Return chicken to pan, add bay leaf, and cook in 325°F oven for 1 hour or until chicken is tender. Makes 4 servings.

Sweet-and-Sour Chicken

2 tablespoons soy sauce	1 sweet red pepper (or green pepper), cubed
1 tablespoon cornstarch	
2 whole chicken breasts, halved, skinned, boned, and cut into bite-sized cubes	**Sweet-and-Sour Sauce**
	2 tablespoons brown sugar
1 tablespoon vegetable oil	2 tablespoons vinegar
1 cucumber, scored lengthwise with tines of fork, cut into bite-sized cubes	½ cup pineapple juice (unsweetened)
	1 tablespoon cornstarch in 2 tablespoons cold water
½ cantaloupe, seeded, rinded, and cut into bite-sized pieces	3 ounces blanched whole almonds

Combine soy sauce and cornstarch. Coat chicken pieces thoroughly. Heat oil in large frying pan (or wok); stir-fry chicken 3 to 4 minutes. Add cucumber, cantaloupe, and pepper.

Mix sauce ingredients together; add to chicken mixture. Heat, stirring often, until sauce boils and ingredients are heated through. Add almonds. Makes 4 servings.

Chicken Pilaf

Chicken Surprise Parcels

4 **chicken drumsticks**	¼ **cup mushrooms, sliced**
Salt and pepper	1 **tablespoon lemon juice**
Worcestershire sauce	4 **tablespoons margarine**
1 **onion, peeled and sliced**	

Wipe chicken and season with salt and pepper. Place each drumstick in the center of a square of foil and sprinkle with Worcestershire sauce. Put onion and mushrooms on top, sprinkle with lemon juice, then dot with margarine. Close foil parcels, using double folds. Place on a baking tray and cook in 400°F oven for about 40 minutes or until chicken is tender. Fold back foil for the last 10 minutes to allow chicken to brown. Serve in the foil. Makes 4 servings.

Chicken and Taco-Chips Casserole

9 **taco shells or 1 (12-ounce) bag taco chips**	2 **cups sharp Cheddar cheese, grated**
2 **whole chicken breasts, cooked and chopped**	1 **(10-ounce) can tomatoes and green chilies**
1 **(10½-ounce) can condensed chicken-and rice soup**	

Crush taco shells or chips in bowl. Place layer of chips in bottom of greased 1-quart casserole. Sprinkle layer of chicken over chips. Pour several spoonfuls of soup over chicken layer. Sprinkle with layer of cheese. Pour several spoonfuls of tomato and green-chili mixture over cheese layer. Repeat layering process until all ingredients are used. Top casserole with additional grated cheese if desired. Bake 25 minutes at 350°F.

This can be prepared ahead and refrigerated before baking. It freezes well before and after baking. Makes 4 to 6 servings.

Chicken with Tomatoes and Olives

4 **breast quarters of frying chicken**	2 **cups broken-up canned tomatoes**
½ **cup flour**	½ **cup white wine**
2 **tablespoons butter**	1 **teaspoon chili powder**
2 **tablespoons olive oil**	½ **teaspoon ground cumin**
1 **clove garlic, chopped**	½ **teaspoon salt**
1 **cup onion, chopped**	¼ **teaspoon pepper**
¼ **cup carrots, chopped**	¾ **cup cut-up black olives**
¼ **cup celery, chopped**	

Wash chicken; pat dry. Dredge chicken in flour; shake off excess.

Heat butter and oil together in deep skillet or Dutch oven. Brown chicken well on all sides. Remove chicken from pan. Lightly brown garlic, onion, carrots, and celery in pan drippings.

Force tomatoes through sieve or puree in blender or food processor. Add tomatoes and wine to vegetables in pan or skillet. Add seasonings; stir well. Place chicken in sauce. Simmer over low heat 30 minutes or until chicken is tender. Add olives and heat through. Makes 4 servings.

Grilled Chicken with Pineapple

Chicken with Tomato-Wine Sauce

1 **(3-pound) chicken**	1 **clove garlic, crushed**
2 **level tablespoons plain flour**	¼ **cup mushrooms, sliced**
Salt and pepper	2 **carrots, peeled and sliced**
6 **tablespoons oil**	1 **(16-ounce) can tomatoes**
1 **onion, chopped**	2 **tablespoons red wine**

Cut chicken into 8 small pieces. Mix flour with salt and pepper and sprinkle over each chicken piece. Heat oil in a large frying pan and fry chicken until golden; transfer to an ovenproof casserole.

Add onion and garlic to pan and cook until softened. Add mushrooms and carrot, and continue frying, stirring occasionally, until onion is lightly browned. Add tomatoes and wine. Bring to a boil, then pour over chicken. Cover casserole and cook in a 350°F oven about 45 minutes, or until chicken is tender. Makes 4 servings.

Chicken in Wine

1	(3- to 4-pound) chicken, cut into serving pieces
⅓	cup vegetable oil
¼	cup cognac
2	medium onions, quartered
1	clove garlic, minced
3	cups Burgundy wine
¼	teaspoon thyme
½	tablespoon tomato paste
1	bay leaf
½	teaspoon salt
⅛	teaspoon pepper

3	strips bacon, cut into 2-inch strips
1	(4-ounce) can button mushrooms, drained, or ¾ cup small mushrooms, quartered
1	tablespoon butter, softened
1	tablespoon flour
1 or 2	parsley sprigs
2	slices white bread, toasted (optional)

In large Dutch oven, brown chicken in hot oil. Drain fat. Pour in cognac; carefully ignite. When flames subside, add onions, garlic, wine, thyme, tomato paste, bay leaf, salt, and pepper. Bring mixture to a boil; simmer, covered, for 1 hour. Skim off fat; correct seasonings. Discard bay leaf.

Meanwhile, place bacon in frying pan; cook until done. Remove bacon; sauté mushrooms in hot fat. Drain off fat. Keep bacon and mushrooms warm until needed.

Blend butter and flour together to a smooth paste. When chicken is done, add paste to hot liquid. Stir and simmer for a minute or two.

Arrange chicken in casserole or serving dish. Baste with sauce. Garnish with bacon, mushrooms, and parsley. Add toast if desired. Makes 4 servings.

Chicken with Vegetables

1	(3-pound) chicken
	Salt and pepper
3	strips bacon
2	tablespoons corn oil
1	cup shallots or small onions, peeled
1	clove garlic, crushed

2	carrots, sliced
2	sticks celery, chopped
½	cup mushrooms, sliced
1	(8-ounce) can tomatoes
½	cup chicken stock or water and chicken stock cube

Cut chicken into 4 serving portions and sprinkle them with salt and pepper. Chop the bacon. Fry bacon in a large saucepan until softened. Add oil; then fry chicken until golden all over (about 10 minutes).

Remove chicken and fry onions until golden. Add garlic, carrots, celery, and mushrooms; cook, stirring, for 2 to 3 minutes. Add tomatoes and stock. Then return chicken to pan. Cover and cook for about 30 minutes or until chicken is tender.

Remove chicken to a serving plate and keep hot. Bring sauce to a boil and boil rapidly until thickening (about 2 to 3 minutes). Pour over chicken and serve. Makes 4 servings.

Deviled Roast Chicken

Chicken Livers with Apples and Onion

¾ **pound chicken livers**	3 **medium apples**
3 **tablespoons flour**	¼ **cup vegetable oil**
½ **teaspoon salt**	¼ **cup sugar**
¼ **teaspoon pepper**	1 **large onion, thinly sliced**
⅛ **teaspoon cayenne pepper**	

Rinse livers; drain on paper towels. Coat evenly with mixture of flour, salt, pepper, and cayenne; set aside.

Wash apples; remove cores. Cut into 1/2-inch slices, to form rings. Heat 2 tablespoons oil in frying pan over medium heat. Add apples; cook until lightly brown. Turn slices carefully; sprinkle with sugar. Cook, uncovered, over low heat until tender. Remove from pan; reserve.

Heat remaining oil over low heat. Add livers and onion rings. Cook over medium heat; turn often to brown all sides.

Transfer to warm serving platter. Serve with apple rings. Makes 4 servings.

Eggs and Chicken Livers

2 **pounds chicken livers**	1 **cup Cheddar cheese, grated**
½ **cup flour seasoned with ½ teaspoon salt and ¼ teaspoon black pepper**	12 **eggs, well beaten**
3 **tablespoons butter**	½ **teaspoon baking powder**
¼ **cup Madeira wine**	½ **pound salted almonds**
4 **large tomatoes, peeled and diced**	

Roll livers in flour.

Melt butter in saucepan; sauté livers. Add wine and tomatoes; simmer about 4 minutes. Transfer liver and wine mixture to 1-1/2-quart casserole. Sprinkle with cheese; broil until cheese melts.

Pour eggs, to which 1/2 teaspoon baking powder has been added, into hot buttered skillet; let cook slowly until eggs become set on bottom of pan. With fork or spatula, lift up eggs at edge of pan, allowing uncooked egg to run underneath. Continue cooking and lifting until eggs are set. Place eggs in center of platter; border with livers. Sprinkle almonds over livers; garnish with parsley. Makes 8 servings.

Chicken Livers Paprikash

1 **pound chicken livers**	1 **tablespoon Hungarian**
4 **tablespoons butter or**	**sweet paprika**
margarine	**Salt and pepper**
1 **cup onions, thinly sliced**	1 **cup chicken broth**
1 **clove garlic, peeled and**	¼ **cup sour cream**
mashed	1 **tablespoon flour**

Rinse livers; drain very well. Remove fat or connective tissue.

Melt butter in large heavy skillet over moderate heat. Add onions and garlic; cook, stirring, until browned. Remove from heat. Add paprika, salt, and pepper; stir well. Add chicken broth; cover. Bring to boil; reduce heat to low. Cook 15 to 20 minutes or until livers are done to taste.

Combine sour cream and flour; stir well. Add slowly to liver mixture, stirring well. Cook over very low heat until thickened.

Serve livers with buttered noodles or dumplings; garnish with chopped parsley. Makes 4 servings.

Chicken Liver Risotto

2 **tablespoons oil**	2 **tablespoons margarine**
1 **onion, peeled and**	¼ **pound mushrooms, sliced**
chopped	½ **pound chicken livers**
2 **strips lean bacon, chopped**	**Chopped parsley for garnish**
1¼ **cups long-grain rice**	**Grated cheese for serving**
2 **cups chicken stock or**	
water and chicken stock	
cube	

Heat oil in a large saucepan. Fry onion and bacon until softened; add rice and cook, stirring, until lightly browned. Add chicken stock and bring to a boil. Cover pan tightly and simmer for 15 minutes. Do not lift lid until end of cooking time, when all liquid is absorbed and rice is tender.

Meanwhile, heat margarine in a frying pan and cook mushrooms and chicken livers until livers are browned all over. Add mushrooms and livers to cooked rice and reheat if necessary. Serve in a hot dish; garnished with chopped parsley. Serve a bowl of grated cheese separately. Makes 4 servings.

Roast Chicken

Chicken Livers on Toast

1	can mushroom gravy	1	pound chicken livers
2	tablespoons sherry	1	egg, beaten
½	cup flour	4	or more tablespoons butter
½	teaspoon dried dillweed		or margarine

Mix gravy and sherry in saucepan; bring to boil. Lower heat; simmer 5 minutes.

Combine flour and dillweed for batter. Put each liver into beaten egg, then into flour. Be sure to coat all sides of livers well.

Melt butter in medium skillet. Add livers; cook over moderate heat 10 minutes or until golden brown. Serve on toast squares with hot gravy. Makes 4 servings.

Turkey Dishes

Curried Turkey

1½ cups cooked turkey
Juice of ½ lemon
4 tablespoons margarine
1 clove garlic, crushed
½ level teaspoon ground ginger
1 onion, chopped
1 level tablespoon plain flour
1 level tablespoon curry powder, or to taste

1 cup chicken stock or water and chicken stock cube
1 tablespoon tomato puree
1 small dessert apple, peeled, cored, and chopped
1 tablespoon raisins
Pinch of sugar
Salt and pepper

Cut turkey into bite-sized pieces and mix with lemon juice in a bowl. Heat margarine in a saucepan; add garlic, ginger, onion, flour, and curry powder. Fry gently, stirring, for 3 to 4 minutes. Stir in chicken stock; bring to a boil. Add tomato puree, apple, raisins, sugar, and salt and pepper to taste. Cover pan and simmer for 15 minutes. Stir in the turkey and cook for a further 10 minutes. Makes 4 servings.

Turkey and Mushroom Croquettes

5 **tablespoons butter**	3 to 4 **tablespoons**
4 **tablespoons flour**	**mushrooms, chopped**
½ **cup strong turkey or**	**Little lemon juice**
chicken stock	1 **egg yolk, beaten**
½ **cup milk**	½ **cup seasoned flour**
Salt and pepper	2 **eggs, beaten with 1**
Pinch of mace	**teaspoon oil**
Small pinch of cayenne pepper	1 to 1½ **cups dried white**
1 **tablespoon parsley,**	**bread crumbs**
chopped	**Fat for deep frying**
2 **cups cooked turkey,**	
chopped	

Make thick sauce. Melt 4 tablespoons butter; add 4 tablespoons flour. Add stock and milk and bring to boil. Cook until thick and smooth. Add seasonings and parsley; let cool.

Meanwhile, chop turkey into small pieces. Chop mushrooms; cook in 1 tablespoon butter. Sprinkle with lemon juice. Add chopped turkey, then sauce, and stir well. When almost cold, add egg yolk; put into refrigerator to chill and set.

Divide into 12 equal portions; shape each into small roll with floured fingers. Roll in seasoned flour, coating ends carefully. Brush all over with beaten egg; cover thickly with bread crumbs.

Heat fat to 390°F or smoking hot. Fry 4 croquettes at a time until well browned; drain well. Serve at once with a piquant brown or tomato sauce. Makes 4 to 6 servings.

Turkey Noodle Ring

½ **pound noodles**	2 **tablespoons flour**
5 to 7 **tablespoons butter**	½ **cup stock**
1 **onion, chopped**	¾ **cup milk**
1 **clove garlic**	2 **cups cooked turkey,**
1 **cup whipping cream**	**chopped**
1 **egg**	¼ **cup cooked peas and corn**
3 to 4 **tablespoons Cheddar**	2 **tablespoons cooked**
cheese, grated	**pimiento, chopped**
1 **tablespoon chopped herbs**	2 **hard-boiled eggs,**
Salt and pepper	**quartered**
2 **onions, finely sliced**	**Pinch of paprika**
1 **cup mushrooms**	

Spring Chicken Casserole

Boil noodles in plenty of salted water until almost cooked; drain.

Heat 3 to 4 tablespoons butter in pan; cook chopped onion and garlic a few minutes to soften. Stir in noodles. Add cream beaten with egg, cheese, and herbs. Sprinkle liberally with salt and pepper; mix thoroughly. Turn into buttered ring mold; press in well. Cover with buttered paper. Put in preheated 350°F oven 45 minutes to set and to finish cooking noodles. Remove when done. Turn out on hot dish; fill with turkey filling.

Melt 2 to 3 tablespoons butter; cook sliced onions 5 to 6 minutes to soften. Add mushrooms, stirring well. Sprinkle in flour and blend well. Add stock and milk; bring to boil. Simmer 4 to 5 minutes, then remove from heat. Add turkey, peas and corn, pimiento, and hard-boiled eggs. Season well; let stand in warm place until noodle ring is ready. Spoon into center; sprinkle with paprika. Makes 4 servings.

Turkey Loaf

2 **eggs**	2 **tablespoons flour**
1 **generous cup cooked turkey, ham, and stuffing (as available)**	1 **cup milk**
½ **pound bacon**	**Salt and pepper to taste**
2 **tablespoons margarine**	**Watercress and tomatoes for garnish**

Cook eggs in boiling water to cover for 10 minutes. Cool in cold water; crack the shells.

Cut turkey, ham, and stuffing into small pieces. Remove any small bones. Using the back of a knife, stretch bacon strips until they are doubled in length. Arrange bacon over the base and sides of a 1-pound capacity loaf tin. Reserve some bacon strips for the top.

Melt margarine in a saucepan, add flour, and cook gently, stirring, for 2 to 3 minutes. Blend in milk. Bring to a boil, stirring constantly; then add salt and pepper. Stir in the prepared turkey, ham, and stuffing.

Put 1/2 the mixture into the loaf pan, place eggs on top, and cover with remaining mixture. Press down firmly. Cover with reserved bacon. Cover pan with foil and place it in a larger tin with enough water to come halfway up the sides. Bake in a 350°F oven for 1 hour. Leave loaf in pan to cool, then chill in refrigerator. Turn loaf out onto a serving plate and garnish with watercress and tomatoes. Makes 4 servings.

Turkey-and-Broccoli Casserole

2 **packages frozen broccoli, cooked**	1 **cup dry white wine**
⅓ **cup butter**	**Salt and pepper**
⅓ **cup flour**	**Worcestershire sauce**
1½ **cups turkey broth or consommé**	3 **cups cooked turkey or chicken, coarsely diced**
1 **cup evaporated milk**	**Grated Parmesan cheese**

Arrange broccoli in greased shallow casserole dish.

Melt butter; stir in flour. Add broth, milk, and wine. Cook, stirring constantly, until mixture is thickened and smooth. Cook and stir 2 or 3 minutes. Season to taste.

Lay turkey over broccoli in baking dish. Cover with wine-cream sauce. Sprinkle generously with grated cheese. Bake at 400°F about 20 minutes or until bubbly. Makes 6 to 8 servings.

Chicken Surprise Parcels

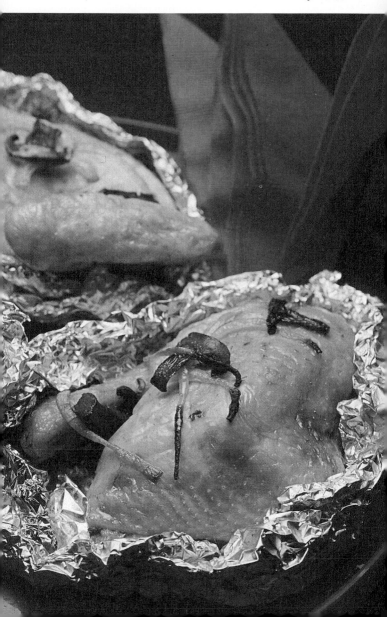

Roast Turkey with Blue-Cheese Sauce

1 (12-pound) turkey	1 cup half-and-half cream
Salt and freshly ground pepper	3 tablespoons all-purpose
Butter	flour
20 medium onions, peeled	1 tablespoon red currant
2 tablespoons soy sauce	jelly
½ cup onions, chopped	1 tablespoon blue cheese

Cut tips from turkey wings. Rub turkey generously inside and out with salt and pepper; brush with melted butter. Tie legs together; place on 1 side on rack in roasting pan. Place wing tips, neck, heart, liver, gizzard, and whole onions around whole turkey in bottom of pan. Roast in preheated 350°F oven 30 minutes; remove turkey pieces. Roast whole turkey 30 minutes longer.

Place turkey pieces in large saucepan. Add 4 cups water and soy sauce.

Sauté chopped onions in small amount of butter until transparent; add to soy-sauce mixture. Bring to boil; boil, uncovered, over medium heat until liquid is reduced to about 2 cups broth. Strain broth; set aside.

Turn turkey to other side; brush with butter. Roast 1 hour. Turn turkey breast-side-up; roast 1 hour longer or until brown and tender. Remove turkey and onions to serving platter.

Pour pan drippings into bowl to cool. Remove fat from surface; reserve 2 tablespoons. Strain drippings. Combine 1 cup drippings, reserved broth, and cream.

Place reserved fat in medium saucepan; blend in flour until smooth. Add cream mixture gradually; cook, stirring constantly, until sauce is smooth and thickened. Add jelly and blue cheese; cook, stirring, until blended. Carve turkey; serve with sauce and additional currant jelly. Makes about 10 servings.

Turkey Pot Roast

1 turkey hindquarter (about 2 pounds)	3 medium potatoes, pared and halved
Salt and pepper to taste	6 medium carrots, scraped
½ cup onion, peeled and finely chopped	and cut into chunks
2 small cloves garlic	1 tablespoon cornstarch
½ teaspoon crumbled dried basil	¼ cup cold water
¼ teaspoon dried thyme	2 tablespoons fresh parsley, chopped
1 cup fat-skimmed turkey broth or water	

Chicken with Tomato-Wine Sauce

Place turkey skin-side-up in nonstick Dutch oven. Salt and pepper to taste. Bake in preheated 450°F oven 20 to 25 minutes, until skin is crisp. Drain; discard any fat.

Add onion, garlic, basil, thyme, and broth; cover. Simmer over low heat (or bake at 350°F) until turkey is nearly tender, about 1 hour. Add potatoes and carrots; cover. Cook until vegetables are tender, about 20 minutes. Remove turkey and vegetables to platter; keep warm. Skim fat from pan juices; discard.

Stir cornstarch and cold water together; add to simmering pan juices. Cook, stirring, until sauce is thickened. Spoon over turkey and vegetables; garnish with parsley. Makes about 6 servings.

Barbecued Turkey

½ cup onion, chopped	1 teaspoon salt
1½ tablespoons butter	¼ teaspoon freshly ground pepper
1½ cups catsup	
¼ cup brown sugar, packed	1 (12-pound) fresh or frozen turkey
1 clove garlic, pressed	
1 lemon, thinly sliced	2 to 3 tablespoons barbecue or seasoned salt
¼ cup Worcestershire sauce	
2 teaspoons prepared mustard	

Sauté onion in butter in small saucepan until lightly browned. Add remaining ingredients, except turkey and barbecue salt; simmer 20 minutes. Remove lemon slices. Store sauce in covered jar in refrigerator if not used immediately.

Thaw turkey, if frozen. Rinse; pat dry.

Start charcoal fire 20 to 30 minutes before cooking turkey, allowing about 5 pounds charcoal for beginning fire. During cooking period, push burning charcoal to center; add more briquettes as needed around edge.

Sprinkle cavity of turkey with barbecue salt. Insert split rod in front of tail; run diagonally through breastbone. Fasten tightly with spit forks at both ends. Test for balance; readjust spit rod, if necessary. Insert meat thermometer into thickest part of inside thigh; make sure thermometer does not touch bone or spit rod and that thermometer will clear charcoal as spit turns.

Brush off gray ash from coals; push coals back of firebox. Place drip pan made of heavy-duty foil directly under turkey in front of coals. Attach spit; start rotisserie. Cook 25 minutes per pound or 180 to 185°F on meat thermometer; baste generously and frequently with barbecue sauce during last 30 minutes of cooking. Makes 10 to 12 servings.

Turkey Tetrazzini

6 tablespoons butter or margarine	¾ cup Parmesan cheese, grated
3 tablespoons olive oil	⅛ teaspoon ground nutmeg
½ pound fresh mushrooms, cleaned and sliced	3 cups cooked turkey, cubed
4 tablespoons flour	½ pound spaghetti or vermicelli, cooked and drained
2 cups chicken broth	
1 cup heavy cream	¼ cup Italian-style bread crumbs
2 tablespoons dry sherry	

Heat 4 tablespoons butter and oil in large saucepan. Add mushrooms; sauté 5 minutes. Remove mushrooms with slotted spoon; reserve.

Add flour to pan juices; stir to form roux. Cook until bubbly. Slowly add broth and cook until thickened. Remove from heat. Add cream, sherry, Parmesan, and nutmeg; stir until cheese melts. Add turkey and mushrooms; stir well. Combine with cooked spaghetti. Turn into greased 13 x 9 x 2-inch baking dish (or 3-quart baking dish).

Melt 2 tablespoons butter, then add bread crumbs. Sprinkle over casserole. Bake in preheated 375°F oven 25 to 30 minutes. Makes 6 servings.

Roast Turkey with Chestnut Dressing

1	(10- to 12-pound) turkey, thawed if frozen	¾	teaspoon salt
			Freshly ground black pepper
		½	teaspoon Hungarian sweet paprika
Chestnut Dressing			
¼	cup butter or margarine	6	cups soft bread cubes
1	large onion, peeled and chopped	¼	cup parsley, chopped
2	stalks celery, chopped	1	pound chestnuts, roasted, skinned, and chopped
¼	pound ground veal	1	egg, well beaten
¼	pound ground pork	5	slices bacon
1	turkey liver, chopped		

Wash turkey well; drain. Remove giblet pack; save liver for dressing. Lightly salt cavity of turkey; set aside while preparing dressing.

Melt butter in large skillet. Add onion and celery; sauté until tender. Using slotted spoon, transfer to large mixing bowl.

Add veal, pork, and liver to skillet; sauté until lightly browned. Season with salt, pepper, and paprika; add to onion mixture. Add remaining stuffing ingredients and mix well.

Stuff turkey with dressing; truss. Place in roasting pan, breast-side up. Lay bacon strips in single layer over turkey. Roast in preheated 325°F oven approximately 4 hours, to internal temperature of 185°F. Let stand, tented with aluminum foil, 20 minutes before carving.

Make a favorite gravy with pan drippings. Makes 6 to 8 servings.

Roast Turkey with Fruit Stuffing

1 (14-pound) turkey	**Sugar to taste**
Salt and pepper	**6** strips bacon
3 pounds cooking apples	**1** pound sausages
⅔ cup prunes	**Watercress for garnish**
¼ pound margarine	

Prepare turkey: Wipe inside with a damp cloth and season with salt and pepper. Peel, core, and slice apples.

Chop prunes coarsely; remove stones. Melt 1/2 the margarine in a saucepan; add apple, cover pan, and cook gently until apple is tender. Occasionally shake pan gently to prevent apple from sticking. Stir in prunes and sugar to taste. Cool, then spoon stuffing into turkey.

Truss turkey, then rub outside with remaining margarine. Roast in a 375°F oven for 15 minutes per pound plus 15 minutes over. If the bird becomes over-brown, place a piece of foil over the breast. Stretch bacon with the back of a knife until doubled in length. Cut into 2 or 3 pieces, roll up, and put on a skewer. Place bacon rolls and sausages in the roasting pan and cook beside the turkey for the last 30 minutes, or until brown.

Serve turkey on a large dish surrounded with bacon and sausages and garnished with watercress. Makes 18 to 20 servings.

Turkey Timbale

3 tablespoons butter	***Mushroom Sauce***
2 tablespoons flour	**3** tablespoons butter
1 cup milk	**16 to 20 mushrooms,**
1 onion, sliced	**quartered**
1 teaspoon mixed herbs	**2** tablespoons flour
Salt and pepper	**1½** cups well-flavored brown
2 to 3 cups turkey meat, finely	**stock**
chopped	**Salt and pepper**
2 eggs	**1** tablespoon chopped herbs
3 to 4 tablespoons thick cream	**2** teaspoons Worcestershire
	sauce
	2 to 3 tablespoons Madeira or
	sherry

Make thick cream sauce. Melt 2 tablespoons butter; stir in flour until blended. Strain in milk, previously heated with onion and herbs; bring to boil, stirring constantly. Cook a few minutes. Add seasoning; let cool.

Grind turkey finely in blender or food processor; mix with eggs beaten in cream. Add cooled cream sauce and mix well. Turn into thoroughly buttered ring mold; allow a little space at top for expansion while cooking.

Chicken with Vegetables

Cover with buttered paper; put in roasting pan of hot water. Bake in preheated 350°F oven 25 to 35 minutes, until skewer inserted in center comes out clean.

Make mushroom sauce while timbale cooks. Melt butter; cook mushrooms 2 to 3 minutes. Sprinkle in flour; cook 1 minute. Remove from heat. Add stock and blend thoroughly. Bring to boil, then simmer a few minutes. Add seasoning, herbs, Worcestershire sauce, and Madeira; let flavors blend well.

Run knife around outside and inner ring of mold; turn onto large round plate. Pour mushroom sauce into center; serve at once. Makes 4 servings.

Chicken Liver Risotto

Turkey Slices on Vegetable Bed

1 **tablespoon butter or margarine**	2 **tablespoons parsley, chopped**
8 **ounces fresh small mushrooms**	½ **teaspoon salt**
2 **(10-ounce) packages frozen peas, defrosted**	2 **tablespoons vegetable oil**
4 **small tomatoes, peeled and halved**	4 **thick slices cooked turkey breast**
	Seasonings to taste

Melt butter in 2-quart saucepan. Add mushrooms; sauté lightly. Add peas; cover. Heat gently 3 minutes. Add tomatoes and parsley; simmer 3 minutes. Season with salt.

Heat oil in separate pan; sauté turkey 2 to 3 minutes on each side or until golden brown. Season to taste.

Arrange vegetables on heated platter. (Use slotted spoon if too much liquid has accumulated.) Arrange turkey slices on vegetables. Makes 4 servings.

Other Fowl

Apricot Duck

1	(4- to 5-pound) roasting duck
1	pound fresh apricots (or 1 large can, drained), seeded
1	orange
1	onion, finely chopped
Salt and pepper	

2 to 3 tablespoons oil	
3	tablespoons honey
1 to 1½ cups stock made with duck giblets (or chicken bouillon cube)	
3 to 4 tablespoons apricot brandy	

Stuff duck with 1/2 of the apricots and 3 strips of orange zest (the thin outer skin of orange), onion, and seasoning. Prick skin of duck with fork to allow fat to run out while cooking; season with pepper and salt.

Heat oil in roasting pan. When very hot, add duck; baste all over with oil. Roast in preheated 400°F oven; allow 20 minutes per pound. Half an hour before cooking is completed, spoon melted honey and juice of orange over duck, to give skin shiny crispness. Ten minutes before end of cooking, add rest of apricots to pan; heat through and brown slightly. Remove duck to warm dish; remove stuffing to bowl. Arrange roasted apricots around duck.

Pour off fat from roasting pan. Put in stuffing; bring to boil, stirring all the time. Taste for seasoning. Strain or blend in liquidizer, blender, or food processor. Return to heat; add apricot brandy. Serve at once with duck and apricots. Makes 4 to 6 servings.

Boned Duck with Orange Stuffing

1 (5-pound) duck	½ cup soft white bread
Salt and pepper	crumbs
4 tablespoons margarine	1 orange
1 large onion, chopped	1 teaspoon orange rind
4 sticks celery, finely	Beaten egg to mix
chopped	Watercress for garnish
¾ pound sausage	
¼ level teaspoon ground	
nutmeg	

Bone duck or ask your butcher to do this for you. Season inside with salt and pepper. Melt margarine in a saucepan and fry onion and celery until soft and golden. Stir in sausage, nutmeg, bread crumbs, 1 teaspoon finely grated orange rind, and enough egg to bind.

Peel orange and cut into quarters. Place 1/3 of the stuffing in the duck. Arrange orange quarters evenly on top, then cover with remaining stuffing. Make duck into a neat parcel and sew opening together with fine string.

Place duck on a rack in a roasting pan and cook in a 375°F oven for 2 hours. Cover duck with foil if it becomes too brown. Serve hot or cold, garnished with watercress. Makes 8 to 10 servings.

Roast Duck with Celery Stuffing

1 (4-pound) duck	½ cup milk
Salt and pepper	2 tablespoons parsley,
¼ pound streaky bacon,	chopped
chopped	¼ teaspoon each dried sage
Liver from the duck	and thyme
2 onions, chopped	Beaten egg to bind
2 sticks celery, chopped	Extra celery, canned cherries,
1 cup soft white bread	and watercress for garnish
crumbs	

Prepare duck; wipe inside with a clean damp cloth. Sprinkle with salt and pepper. Fry bacon in a saucepan; add liver, then chop when cooked. Fry the onions and celery until soft, then stir in the bread crumbs, milk, herbs, salt and pepper, and enough beaten egg to bind. Pile the stuffing into the duck and truss. Roast the duck in a 375°F oven for 15 minutes per pound plus 15 minutes over.

To prepare the garnish, cut some celery into 1-inch lengths; cook in boiling salted water until tender. Heat the cherries in their own syrup. Place the duck on a large serving dish and arrange the garnish around it. Add watercress to complete the garnish. Makes 4 servings.

Curried Turkey

Duck Savoyarde

2	(4- to 5-pound) ducks
6	tablespoons unbleached flour
2	teaspoons salt
½	teaspoon black pepper
½	teaspoon paprika
½	teaspoon oregano
2	tablespoons oil
2	tablespoons butter or margarine
¾	pound mushrooms, sliced
4	onions, peeled and quartered

6	carrots, scraped and cut into large strips
1	clove garlic, crushed (optional)
2 to 3 cups red wine
10	ripe olives, chopped

Garnish
Red currant jam or guava jelly
Parsley sprigs
Wild or savory rice

Have butcher clean ducks and disjoint them into 6 or 8 pieces each. Place pieces in paper or plastic bag with flour and seasonings; shake until well coated.

Heat oil and butter in large skillet. Brown ducks on all sides; transfer to large casserole as they are browned.

In same skillet, brown mushrooms, onions, carrots, and garlic; add more oil and butter if necessary. Add mixture to ducks. Add wine; cover. Bake at 350°F 1 hour. Fifteen minutes before end of cooking time, add olives.

Remove ducks from casserole to heated platter. Remove as much fat as possible from sauce in pan. Pour sauce over ducks. Garnish platter with sprigs of parsley. Serve with red currant or guava jelly and wild or savory rice. Makes 8 or more servings.

Brandied Duck

1	(5- to 6-pound) duck
2	large onions, chopped
¼	cup parsley, minced
1	bay leaf
½	teaspoon thyme
2	cloves garlic, crushed

3	jiggers brandy
2	cups red wine
¼	cup olive oil or butter
¾	pound mushrooms, sliced
Salt
Pepper

Clean duck, then cut it into serving pieces. Place in deep dish. Add onions, parsley, bay leaf, thyme, garlic cloves, brandy, and wine to duck. Marinate at least 4 hours, preferably overnight.

Heat oil; brown pieces of duck about 15 minutes. Add marinade, mushrooms, and seasonings. Cover tightly; simmer over low heat at least 1 hour. Makes 4 to 6 servings.

Turkey Loaf

Duckling with Oranges

¼ **cup olive oil**	**Strips of peel of 1 orange and**
¼ **cup butter**	**1 lemon**
1 **large duckling**	**Juice of 1 orange**
Seasoned flour	**Juice of ½ lemon**
2 **tablespoons wine vinegar**	1 **teaspoon curaçao**
2 **teaspoons sugar**	1 **teaspoon brandy**

Heat oil and butter in large frying pan. Dredge duckling with seasoned flour. Place in pan over medium-high heat; brown on all sides. Place in heavy baking dish. Pour pan drippings over duckling; cover. Bake in pre-heated 350°F oven about 1-1/2 hours or until duckling is tender. Remove duckling from baking dish; place on heated platter. Keep warm. Pour off excess fat from casserole drippings.

Place vinegar and sugar in small saucepan. Cook over low heat, stir-ring, until sugar is dissolved. Stir in drippings, orange and lemon strips, and orange and lemon juice; cook over medium heat until liquid is reduced by half. Add curaçao and brandy; pour over duckling. Makes about 4 servings.

Goose with Chestnut and Liver Stuffing

2 **pounds chestnuts**	**Grated rind of ½ lemon**
2 **cups stock**	**Salt and pepper**
6 **apples**	1 **(8- to 10-pound) goose**
2 **onions, chopped**	2 **tablespoons flour**
1 **goose liver**	4 to 6 **tablespoons oil**
1 **tablespoon butter**	2 **tablespoons red currant**
2 **cups bread crumbs**	**jelly**
2 **tablespoons parsley,**	**Juice of ½ lemon**
chopped	1½ **cups cider or stock**
1 **tablespoon mixed thyme**	
and marjoram	

Prepare stuffing. Put chestnuts in boiling water 5 to 6 minutes, until both outer shell and inner skin can be removed. Keep chestnuts hot while peeling. Cover nuts with stock; simmer until tender. Drain; let cool. Reserve stock for moistening stuffing.

Peel and chop apples. Add onions; cook 3 to 4 minutes. Mix in chestnuts.

Cook liver in butter; when firm, chop; add to stuffing with 1 to 2 cups bread crumbs. Add parsley, thyme, marjoram, lemon rind, salt, and pepper; mix together. Add enough stock to make moist but firm mixture. Stuff goose; sew up opening. Prick goose all over lightly with sharp fork; sprinkle with 1 tablespoon flour and seasoning.

Heat oil in roasting pan. Put goose into pan on rack, if possible, to allow fat to drain; roast in preheated 400°F oven 20 to 25 minutes per pound. Baste every 20 minutes; turn from side to side. Reduce heat slightly after first 20 minutes. For last 30 minutes, pour off most of fat. Place bird breast-up; allow to brown. Raise heat again if breast is not becoming crisp and brown. Test with skewer in thick part of leg to see if cooked. When done, remove to serving dish; keep warm while making gravy.

Skim off remaining fat from roasting pan. Sprinkle in 1 tablespoon flour; blend with roasting juices in pan. Add jelly and lemon juice; stir in well. Add cider; bring to boil. Cook 2 to 3 minutes; strain. Season to taste; serve hot with goose. Makes 6 to 8 servings.

Roast Turkey with Fruit Stuffing

Goose with Potato Stuffing

1	(8- to 9-pound) young goose, thawed if frozen	¼	cup onion, finely chopped
		¼	pound bulk sausage
		¼	cup butter or margarine
Potato Stuffing		1	egg
3	medium potatoes (approximately 1 pound), peeled	½	teaspoon pepper
		1	teaspoon sage leaves, crumbled
1½	teaspoons salt		
¼	pound lean salt pork, diced		

Remove giblets from goose; wash well. Pat dry with paper towels. Salt lightly inside and out; set aside while making stuffing.

Place potatoes in medium saucepan; cover with cold water. Add 1/2 teaspoon salt; bring to boil over moderate heat. Cover; cook on low 20 to 30 minutes or until tender. Drain; place tea towel over pan. Steam gently a few minutes.

Meanwhile, cook salt pork in heavy skillet over moderate heat until lightly browned. Remove with slotted spoon; reserve.

Add onion to skillet and cook until tender. Remove with slotted spoon; add to salt pork.

Add sausage to skillet and cook until lightly browned, breaking into small chunks as sausage cooks. Remove with slotted spoon; add to salt-pork mixture.

Put potatoes through ricer or food mill or mash with potato masher. Combine salt-pork mixture, potatoes, and remaining stuffing ingredients; mix well. Allow to cool.

Stuff goose with potato mixture; truss bird. Place in open roasting pan, breast-side-up, on rack or trivet. Prick well on legs and wing joints to release fat. Roast in preheated 325°F oven 2 to 2-1/2 hours, until leg joint moves easily. Let stand 15 to 20 minutes before carving. Carve; remove dressing to serving dish. Serve with applesauce. Makes 6 servings.

Roast Guinea Hen

2	(2- to 3-pound) dressed guinea hens	2	small onions
1½	teaspoons salt	4	slices country-style bacon, sliced
1	lemon, quartered		

Rub hens inside and out with salt and lemon wedges. Insert an onion in each hen; place bacon over backs of hens.

Roast in 325°F oven 40 minutes back-sides-up.

Turn hens over in roasting pan; rearrange bacon over breasts of hens. Cook 35 to 40 minutes or until fork-tender. Makes 4 servings.

Cornish Hens German-Style

1	**small cornish hen, split, or 2 chicken-breast halves**	**2**	**tablespoons Parmesan cheese, grated**
1	**lemon**	**¼**	**teaspoon ground ginger**
3	**tablespoons cracker crumbs or unseasoned bread crumbs**		**Salt and pepper to taste**

Sprinkle poultry with juice of half the lemon.

Combine crumbs, cheese, ginger, salt, and pepper in paper bag. Add poultry; shake until coated. Arrange poultry skin-side-up on shallow roasting pan. Place in preheated 350°F oven. Bake, without turning, until golden and tender, 45 to 50 minutes. Garnish with thin lemon slices, or serve with lemon wedges (and parsley, if desired). Recipe can be doubled or tripled. Makes 2 servings.

Cornish Hens with Plum Sauce

4	**large Cornish hens**	**1**	**teaspoon Worcestershire sauce**
	Salt and freshly ground pepper to taste	**1½**	**teaspoons prepared mustard**
4	**large oranges**	**⅓**	**cup chili sauce**
1	**(1-pound) can purple plums**	**¼**	**cup soy sauce**
¼	**cup butter**	**1**	**(6-ounce) can frozen lemonade concentrate**
¼	**cup onion, minced**	**¼**	**cup shredded coconut**
1	**teaspoon ginger**		

Cut hens in half lengthwise; sprinkle with salt and pepper. Slice unpeeled oranges; remove seeds. Place in 2 shallow, oblong baking pans. Place 4 hen halves, skin-side-up, in each baking pan on oranges. Bake in preheated 350°F oven 45 minutes.

Drain plums; remove seeds. Mix in blender or food processor until pureed.

Melt butter in medium-sized saucepan; add onion. Cook over low heat, stirring constantly, until onion is golden. Add ginger, Worcestershire sauce, mustard, chili sauce, soy sauce, lemonade, and plums; bring to boil. Stir until lemonade is thawed; reduce heat. Simmer 15 minutes, stirring occasionally. Spoon sauce over hens. Bake 30 to 45 minutes, until hens are tender; baste frequently with plum sauce. Remove hens with orange slices to serving platter; sprinkle with coconut. Serve remaining sauce with hens. Makes 4 to 6 servings.

Roast Cornish Hens with Savory Stuffing

4 **Cornish hens, approximately 1 pound each**	¼ **teaspoon freshly ground pepper**
8 **thick slices home-style white bread**	¾ **cup butter**
1½ **tablespoons parsley flakes**	1 **cup onions, finely chopped**
¾ **teaspoon salt**	4 **livers from Cornish hens**
½ **teaspoon poultry seasoning**	**Salt and pepper**
	3 **tablespoons melted butter**

Remove giblet packs from hens; reserve livers. Wash hens; pat dry.

Cut crusts from bread; cut into 1/2-inch cubes. Place on cookie sheet. Bake at 350°F until golden, stirring occasionally. Remove from oven. Combine with parsley, 3/4 teaspoon salt, poultry seasoning, and 1/4 teaspoon pepper; set aside.

Melt 3/4 cup butter in heavy skillet. Add onions and livers; cook until livers are lightly browned and onions tender. Remove livers; chop. Add livers, onions, and butter from pan to bread cubes; toss to mix well.

Salt and pepper hens lightly. Pack tightly with stuffing; truss. Place in ovenproof baking dish, breast-side-up; brush with melted butter. Roast at 375°F. Turn every 15 minutes; baste with butter and pan juices. Cook a total of 45 minutes to 1 hour, until juices run clear when tip of knife is inserted in hen. Serve hot with wild rice and green vegetable. Makes 4 servings.

Casserole of Pigeons

2 to 4 **young pigeons or squabs (depending on size)**	½ **pound carrots, peeled and sliced**
3 **tablespoons flour**	1 **chicken bouillon cube, crumbled**
Salt and pepper	1¼ **cups water**
¼ **cup butter or margarine**	3 or 4 **tomatoes, peeled and sliced**
1 **onion, peeled and chopped**	1 **bay leaf**

Split pigeons into halves; dredge with flour mixed with a little salt and pepper. Heat butter in sauté pan. Brown pigeons on all sides; remove to casserole.

Add onion and carrots to pan; sauté in remaining fat. Put any remaining flour and bouillon cube into pan, add water and stir until boiling. Pour over contents of casserole. Add tomatoes and bay leaf. Cover; cook in preheated 325°F oven about 2 hours. Remove bay leaf and adjust seasoning before serving.

If pigeons are unavailable, use Cornish hens. Makes 4 servings.

Boned Duck with Orange Stuffing

Pheasant with Grapes and White Wine Sauce

4	tablespoons butter	½	cup white wine
1	pheasant	1½	cups white grapes, seedless if available
2	tablespoons flour		
½	cup clear stock	3.	tablespoons lemon juice

Melt butter in heatproof casserole or Dutch oven; when hot, sauté pheasant gently all over until golden brown. Remove bird.

Add flour, stock, and wine; blend smoothly. Bring to boil; add seasoning. Return bird to casserole; cover. Cook in preheated 350°F oven 35 to 45 minutes, until pheasant is tender; turn during cooking.

Peel grapes by dipping in boiling water a few seconds, then in cold water. Strip skins; if not seedless, remove seeds. Cover with a little lemon juice to prevent browning.

When bird is tender, remove and carve. Place meat on serving dish; keep warm.

Add grapes to sauce; cook couple of minutes. Season to taste and spoon sauce over pheasant. Serve with mashed potatoes and peas or spinach. Makes 4 servings.

Braised Pheasant with Chestnut Puree and Orange

4 to 5 tablespoons butter	1½ cups stock
1 large pheasant	¼ cup cider (or white wine)
2 onions, sliced	3 oranges
2 small carrots, sliced	1 tablespoon mixed herbs
2 or 3 stalks celery, sliced	Salt and pepper
2 tablespoons flour	1 large can chestnut puree

Melt 2 to 3 tablespoons butter in heatproof casserole or Dutch oven. Brown bird slowly all over. Remove bird; keep warm.

Add onions, carrots, and celery; cook until they begin to brown slightly. Add flour; cook a few minutes. Add stock and cider; stir well. Bring to boil; simmer a few minutes. Add zest (outer skin) of 1 orange, herbs, and seasonings. Put pheasant back into casserole; spoon sauce over.

Cover casserole. Put in preheated 350°F oven about 50 minutes, until pheasant is tender. When pheasant is removed from casserole, boil cooking juices; put into liquidizer or blender. When juices are smooth, return to pan; if too thick, add a little extra stock. Season to taste; reheat.

Meanwhile, melt 2 tablespoons butter in pan; add chestnut puree. Heat to soften puree; add 2 to 3 tablespoons stock and seasoning. Keep warm until pheasant is tender; place down center of serving dish. Place carved slices and joints on top; spoon sauce over all.

Remove zest of second orange carefully; cut into thin shreds. Cook in boiling water a few minutes; drain. Put into cold water to restore color. Remove white pith and skin from all oranges with sharp knife; divide into segments. Arrange segments around edge of dish and strips down center. Makes 4 to 6 servings.

Squabs with Water Chestnuts

2 to 4 squabs or young pigeons	1 teaspoon sugar
	Salt and pepper
3 tablespoons flour	1 tablespoon soy sauce
3 tablespoons butter or margarine	1 tablespoon sherry
	2 green onions or 1 shallot, chopped
1 chicken bouillon cube, crumbled	10 water chestnuts, sliced
1½ cups water	

Split squabs in halves; dredge with flour. Heat butter in skillet; brown squabs on all sides. Remove to casserole.

Put remaining flour into skillet with bouillon cube and water; stir until boiling. Add sugar, seasoning, soy sauce, sherry, onions, and water chestnuts; pour over squabs. Cover; cook in preheated 350°F oven 1 to 1-1/4 hours. Makes 4 servings.

Roast Duck with Celery Stuffing

Squabs in Parcels

2	large squabs	2	tablespoons chopped
7	tablespoons butter		parsley, marjoram, and
2	slices bacon		tarragon
1	small can goose- or duck-		Salt and pepper
	liver pâté		Pinch of mace
1	cup mushrooms, chopped	1	tablespoon sherry

Cut each squab in half; brown all over in 3 tablespoons butter with bacon. Cover; roast in preheated 350°F oven 20 minutes. Remove squabs; let cool.

Mix pâté with mushrooms, 4 tablespoons butter, herbs, seasoning, and dash of sherry.

Cut 4 large squares of foil; butter. Place 1/8 of stuffing in center of each square. Place halved squabs on top; spread another 1/8 of mixture over each. Fold foil over birds; seal edges by turning over several times. Turn oven up to 400°F; bake parcels 35 minutes. Serve a parcel per person; open at table to get full effect of aroma. Makes 4 servings.

Squab and Bacon Brochettes

2 or 3 squabs
½ cup red wine
1 onion, chopped
1 tablespoon chopped herbs
Pepper
4 slices bacon
8 to 12 baby onions, peeled
1½ cups stock
8 to 12 baby mushrooms (use stems for sauce)

Brown Sauce
3 tablespoons oil
2 bacon slices, chopped
1 onion, chopped
1 clove garlic, crushed
2 carrots, chopped
2 stalks celery, chopped
Mushroom stems
2 tablespoons flour
Stock
½ cup strained marinade
Salt and pepper

Remove breasts from squabs; cut each into 2 pieces. Put into bowl; cover with wine, chopped onion, herbs, and pepper. Let marinate a few hours.

Cut bacon slices in half; make each into roll. Cook baby onions in 1/2 cup stock 5 minutes; drain. Reserve stock for sauce. Peel mushrooms. Remove stems; reserve for sauce. Remove squab from marinade; dry. Thread ingredients alternately onto skewers.

Make brown sauce. Heat oil; cook bacon, onion, garlic, carrots, celery, and mushroom stems until golden brown. Sprinkle in flour and blend well. Add stock and marinade; bring to boil. Simmer 1/2 hour; strain. Add seasoning.

Heat broiler or barbecue grill; cook brochettes, brushing with butter or oil, about 8 minutes, depending on heat of broiler or grill. Squab must not be overcooked—it becomes tough and tasteless. Serve with boiled rice and brown sauce. Makes 4 servings.

Squab Stuffed and Baked

6 **dressed squabs**	1½ **cups fresh mushrooms,**
1½ **teaspoons salt**	**chopped**
1 **cup celery, chopped**	½ **cup raisins**
½ **cup onion, chopped**	1 **tablespoon parsley, finely**
3 **tablespoons butter**	**chopped**
1½ **cups boiled rice**	¾ **teaspoon marjoram**
6 **tablespoons thawed frozen**	¾ **cup vegetable oil**
orange-juice concentrate	

Sprinkle squab cavities well with 3/4 teaspoon salt.

Sauté celery and onion in butter in large skillet until golden. Stir in rice, 3 tablespoons orange-juice concentrate, mushrooms, raisins, parsley, majoram, and remaining salt; blend thoroughly. Heat through; spoon into squab cavities; truss.

Combine oil and remaining orange juice; blend well.

Arrange squab on rack in roasting pan; brush with oil mixture. Bake in preheated 375°F oven 45 minutes or until squabs are tender; baste frequently with remaining oil mixture. Arrange squabs on serving dish; garnish with parsley and orange slices, if desired. Makes 6 servings.

EQUIVALENT MEASURES

dash = 2 or 3 drops
pinch = amount that can be held
            between ends of thumb &
            forefinger
1 tablespoon = 3 teaspoons
¼ cup = 4 tablespoons
⅓ cup = 5 tablespoons + 1 teaspoon
½ cup = 8 tablespoons
1 cup = 16 tablespoons
1 pint = 2 cups
1 quart = 4 cups
1 gallon = 4 quarts
1 peck = 8 quarts
1 bushel = 4 pecks
1 pound = 16 ounces

KITCHEN METRIC

measurements you will encounter
most often in recipes are: centimeter
(cm), milliliter (ml), gram (g),
kilogram (kg)

cup equivalents (volume):

    ¼   cup = 60 ml
    ⅓   cup = 85 ml
    ½   cup = 125 ml
    ⅔   cup = 170 ml
    ¾   cup = 180 ml
    1   cup = 250 ml
    1¼ cups = 310 ml
    1½ cups = 375 ml
    2   cups = 500 ml
    3   cups = 750 ml
    5   cups = 1250 ml

spoonful equivalents (volume):

    ⅛   teaspoon = .5 ml
    ¼   teaspoon = 1.5 ml
    ½   teaspoon = 3 ml
    ¾   teaspoon = 4 ml
    1   teaspoon = 5 ml
    1   tablespoon = 15 ml
    2   tablespoons = 30 ml
    3   tablespoons = 45 ml

pan sizes (linear & volume):

    1 inch = 2.5 cm
    8-inch square = 20-cm square
    9×13×1½-inch = 20×33×4-cm

10×6×2-inch = 25×15×5-cm
13×9×2-inch = 33×23×5-cm
7½×12×1½-inch = 18×30×4-cm
(above are baking dishes, pans)
9×5×3-inch = 23×13×8-cm
(loaf pan)
10-inch = 25 cm   12-inch = 30-cm
(skillets)
1-quart = 1-liter   2-quart = 2-liter
(baking dishes, by volume)
5- to 6-cup = 1.5-liter
(ring mold)

weight (meat amounts;
can & package sizes):

    1   ounce = 28 g
    ½   pound = 225 g
    ¾   pound = 340 g
    1   pound = 450 g
    1½   pounds = 675 g
    2   pounds = 900 g
    3   pounds = 1.4 kg (in recipes,
           amounts of meat above 2 pounds
           will generally be stated in
           kilograms)
    10   ounces = 280 g
           (most frozen vegetables)
    10½   ounces = 294 g
           (most condensed soups)
    15   ounces = 425 g
           (common can size)
    16   ounces = 450 g
           (common can size)
    1   pound, 24 ounces = 850 g
           (can size)

OVEN TEMPERATURES

275°F = 135°C
300°F = 149°C
325°F = 165°C
350°F = 175°C
375°F = 190°C
400°F = 205°C
425°F = 218°C
450°F = 230°C
500°F = 260°C

Note that Celsius temperatures are
sometimes rounded off to the nearest
reading ending in 0 or 5; the Celsius
thermometer is the same as
Centigrade, a term no longer used.

Index

Balnamoon Skink, 10
Barbecue(d)
    Chicken, Hawaiian, 26
    Chicken, Spicy, 26
    Turkey, 74

Chicken
    à la King, 40
    and Artichoke Hearts, 25
    Balnamoon Skink, 10
    Barbecued, Hawaiian, 26
    Barbecued, Spicy, 26
    Bartender's Hors d'Oeuvres, 6
    with Biscuit Topping, 28
    Breasts, Lemon and Garlic-Filled, 42
    Breasts, Stuffed Athenian, 56
    Casserole, Deviled, 36
    Casserole, Spring, 58
    Cheesy Oven-Fried, 29
    Chowder, 8
    in Cider and Mustard, 31
    Cinnamon Orange, 30
    Cordon Bleu, 30
    Cordon Gold, 32
    Country-Style, 32
    Creole, 34
    Crisp Baked, 24
    Croquettes, 34
    Curry, 33
    Deviled Roast, 53
    Drumsticks with Rice, 36
    Drumsticks, Fried, 6
    Florentine, Breast of, 38
    Giblet Soup, 12
    and Green Peppers and Bamboo
        Shoots in Oyster Sauce, 40
    Grilled with Pineapple, 52
    Italian-Style, 38
    Kampama, 39
    Marinated, 42
    Maryland, 44
    Mediterranean, 43
    in Mint Sauce, 44
    Mustard, 45

    Normandy, 46
    and Orange Kebabs, 47
    Oregano Grilled, 46
    Paella, 48
    Paprika, 49
    Parmesan with Mushroom Marsala
        Sauce, 49
    Pâté Cream, 5
    Pie with Herb Topping, 50
    Pilaf, 50
    in Potato Nest, 51
    Rice Casserole, 52
    Roast, 54
    Salad, Avocado and, 17
    Salad, Breasts with Celery, 18
    Salad, Creamy, 18
    Salad, Curried, 20
    Salad, Sorrento, 20
    Salad, Waldorf, 19
    Skewers, 54
    Soup, Irish-Style, 13
    Soup, Noodle, 12
    Spicy Roast, 55
    Stew, 56
    Stew, Brunswick, 28
    Stuffed Apples, 16
    Surprise Parcels, 59
    Sweet-and-Sour, 58
    and Taco-Chips Casserole, 60
    with Tomato-Wine Sauce, 61
    and Tomatoes and Olives, 60
    with Vegetables, 62
    in Wine, 62
    Wings with Oyster Sauce, 8
Cornish Hens
    German-Style, 87
    with Plum Sauce, 87
    Roast with Savory Stuffing, 88
Croquettes
    Chicken, 34
    Turkey, and Mushroom, 68
Curry
    Chicken, 33
    Turkey, 67

Duck
  Apricot, 79
  Boned with Orange Stuffing, 80
  Brandied, 82
  Duckling with Oranges, 83
  Roast with Celery Stuffing, 80
  Savoyarde, 82

Goose
  with Chestnut and Liver Stuffing, 84
  with Potato Stuffing, 86
Gravy, 22
  Giblet, 23
Guinea Hen, Roast, 86

Hen(s)
  Cornish with Plum Sauce, 87
  Cornish, German-Style, 87
  Cornish, Roast with Savory Stuffing,
    88
  Guinea, Roast, 86
Hors d'Oeuvres, Bartender's, 6

Liver, Chicken
  with Apple and Onion, 64
  Broth with Liver Dumplings, 10
  Eggs and, 64
  Giblet Soup, 12
  on Toast, 66
  Paprikash, 65
  Pâté Cream, 5
  Pâté, 8
  Risotto, 65
  and Sausage Pâté, Hot, 6
  Wrapped in Bacon, 11

Pâté
  Chicken Cream, 5
  Chicken-Liver, 8
  Chicken Liver and Sausage, Hot, 6
Pheasant
  Braised with Chestnut Puree and
    Orange, 91
  with Grapes and White Wine Sauce,
    89
Pigeons, Casserole of, 88

Salad
  Avocado and Chicken, 17
  Chicken Breasts and Celery, 18
  Chicken, Creamy, 18
  Chicken, Curried, 20
  Chicken, Waldorf, 19
  Chicken-Stuffed Apples, 16
  Sorrento, 20
  Turkey, Celery, Grape, and Nut, 22
Soup
  Balnamoon Skink, 10
  Broth with Liver Dumplings, 10
  Chicken Chowder, 8
  Chicken Noodle, 12
  Chicken, Irish-Style, 13
  Giblet, 12
  Turkey and Chestnut, Leftover-Style,
    14
  Turkey-Vegetable, 14
Squab(s)
  and Bacon Brochettes, 92
  in Parcels, 92
  Stuffed and Baked, 93
  with Water Chestnuts, 91
Stew
  Brunswick, 28
  Chicken, 56

Turkey
  Barbecued, 74
  and Broccoli Casserole, 70
  Croquettes, and Mushroom, 68
  Curried, 67
  Noodle Ring, 68
  Loaf, 70
  Pot Roast, 72
  Roast with Blue-Cheese Sauce, 72
  Roast with Chestnut Dressing, 75
  Roast with Fruit Stuffing, 76
  Salad, Celery, Grape, and Nut, 22
  Slices on Vegetable Bread, 78
  Soup Leftover-Style, and Chestnut,
    14
  Soup, Vegetable, 14
  Tetrazzini, 74
  Timbale, 76